It *Is* About You

Living Fully, Living Free Through the
Creative Power of Your Thought

It *Is* About You

*Living Fully, Living Free Through the
Creative Power of Your Thought*

A Workbook for Using Spiritual Mind Treatment to
Experience Health, Happiness, Abundance and Peace

Kathy Juline

With selections from the writings of
Ernest Holmes
Founder of the Science of Mind

A revised, updated, and expanded edition of *You Are the One*
Mary M. Jaeger and Kathy Juline

Science of Mind Publications
Golden, Colorado

The material in this book is adapted from the writings of Ernest Holmes, founder of the Science of
Mind teaching and author of *The Science of Mind*.

It Is About You is a revised, updated and expanded edition of
You Are the One © 1988 Science of Mind Publications.

Quotations from contemporary spiritual teachers at the beginning of each of the life areas
are excerpted from interviews appearing in *Science of Mind* magazine, a publication of
United Centers for Spiritual Living, Golden, Colorado.

The printing and production of this work is the result, in whole or in part,
of a grant from the Hefferlin Foundation, a nonprofit religious corporation dedicated
to the promulgation and growth of the Science of Mind as formulated by Ernest Holmes.

Printed in USA
ISBN13: 978-0-9727184-8-6
ISBN10: 0-9727184-8-6

Published by
Science of Mind Publishing
Golden, Colorado

Book design by Randall Friesen

Acknowledgments

Dr. Ernest S. Holmes, founder of the Science of Mind teaching and author of *The Science of Mind*, is the inspiration for this workbook. We gratefully acknowledge him for all that he has given us, including the spiritual practice that he called spiritual mind treatment. All other teachers and students of the Science of Mind are also acknowledged for all that they contribute to our world.

A special acknowledgment is extended to Amanda Pisani of Science of Mind Publishing for her valuable role in the publication of this book.

Gratitude is also extended to members of the Dr. John and Marian Hefferlin Foundation Board, who generously provided the funding for this book.

CONTENTS

PART THREE: LIFE AREAS WORKBOOK

PART FOUR: CONCLUSION

WELCOME TO *It Is About You*

In *It Is About You,* you are beginning the journey toward a new way of living. The one single purpose of this workbook is to help you to heal your life.

Awaiting you is the discovery that through the use of an approach to healing and renewal called spiritual mind treatment, you can change your life for the better. You can attract into your life the good you desire.

If spiritual mind treatment is new to you, be open to it. Developed by Ernest Holmes, founder of the Science of Mind teaching, spiritual mind treatment is a practical application of universal laws. It is a way of recognizing the truth of your spiritual nature and letting it come forth. If spiritual mind treatment is not a new idea to you, allow this workbook to guide you in using spiritual mind treatment to express Spirit more fully in every area of your life.

As you work with the tool of spiritual mind treatment presented in *It Is About You,* your life will be gradually and positively transformed. This happens because you are becoming aware of your true spiritual nature and allowing it to express more fully in your daily experience.

Know that you can change your life for the better by realizing your unity with Spirit and by consciously directing the creative power within you.

It *is* about you. Enjoy your journey!

"To hold one's thought steadfastly to the constructive, to that which endures, and to the Truth, may not be easy in a rapidly changing world, but to the one who makes the attempt much is guaranteed."

—Ernest Holmes

PART ONE
Change Your Thinking, Change Your Life

INTRODUCTION

"If you will take time daily to sense the presence of life within you, to believe in it, to accept it, undesirable experiences which you have had will gradually disappear and something new will be born—a bigger, better, and more perfect you. You will pass from lack and want into greater freedom, from fear into faith. From a sense of being alone, you will pass into the realization of oneness with everything, and you will rejoice."

The above words, written by Ernest Holmes, founder of the Science of Mind philosophy, describe what this workbook is designed to help you to do.

It Is About You is based on the Science of Mind philosophy, which was developed by Ernest Holmes in the early part of the twentieth century and is now taught and practiced worldwide. This philosophy is set forth in his classic book, *The Science of Mind.*

The Science of Mind philosophy teaches that when you establish within yourself a deep awareness of your unity with the presence and power of Spirit, and you apply that awareness to your specific needs, a change in the circumstances of your life occurs. You begin to experience a greater good when you focus on the spiritual truth about yourself rather than on a perception of a problem or need.

Basic to the Science of Mind is a recognition that Spirit is the infinite source and essence of all that exists. By establishing in your mind an awareness of your unity with Spirit and recognizing that awareness as the truth about a specific need in your life, healing occurs. Wholeness is realized in place of lack or limitation. You experience the presence of Spirit in some specific way or form, such as a smoother flow of everyday events and activities, a higher sense of purpose and value to your life, greater physical health or more harmonious relationships with others.

Realizing your unity with the universal allows the wholeness that is the essence of the universal to be more fully expressed in your life.

It Is About You guides you in applying the Science of Mind teaching that problems result from a belief in lack and limitation and that problems are healed when that belief is replaced with an awareness and acceptance of your unity with Spirit. When you embrace new, life-affirming beliefs, you change your life for the better.

How the Creative Principle Works

There is a universal law of Mind, or creative principle, which acts upon your thought to produce an outer effect in accordance with that thought. This idea is the cornerstone of the Science of Mind teaching.

Your thought has creative power because your mind is connected with universal Mind. You are a center in the creative field of Mind. Thus your life experience is a reflection of your inner state of mind. What you are thinking matters. You are always experiencing the effect of the way you think, feel and believe. Your thoughts take shape and form as the everyday conditions and circumstances of your life.

Focusing attention on lack or limitation produces a like experience. When you shift your attention away from lack or limitation and focus instead on what is ultimately true about you, such as the spiritual qualities of health, abundance and peace, accepting these qualities as who you are, you experience health, abundance and peace in your life. This is the basic idea of the Science of Mind.

"There is one life, that life is God, that life is perfect, and that life is your life now." This statement by Ernest Holmes explains why healing is possible. There is one infinite being that is the essence of all that exists. Infinite being is whole and perfect, and it is the totality of the universe. It is the ultimate reality in, as, and through everything. It is your true nature. It is who you are.

Spirit, infinite intelligence, the universal, truth, God, the absolute—all of these terms refer to a principle of unity or oneness that encompasses all and is the source of all, that is present in, as, and through everything.

You are immersed in and connected with the one infinite being. It is your source as well as your own true nature. You partake of and possess the qualities of Spirit. You are an individualized center in Spirit.

Spirit, the Formless Source and Cause of All

Ernest Holmes wrote that when we use words such as God or Spirit, "We are saluting the Divine Presence in each other and in everything—the beauty that sees and imagines and paints the glory of a sunset or the softness of an early dawn, the aroma of the rose, the enthusiasm of a child at play, the intelligence of the philosopher, the worshipful attitude of the devotee. This is all God."

In these words Dr. Holmes beautifully describes that ineffable something that has been known and experienced by mystics, sages and saints of all time.

Spiritual teachings throughout the ages, including the Science of Mind, have recognized a threefold nature to reality, or the universal allness. The presence of Spirit is the guiding idea behind all that exists. It is the "knowing" side of life. Spirit as the idea or the essence, is the formless source and cause of all that exists.

Mind, or law, is the automatic, responsive activity of the universal allness. It is the "doing" side of life. This doing side of life is the creative power of Mind and it operates in accordance with an unfailing law that responds to the pattern presented to it. Your thoughts—including your feelings and beliefs—make up this pattern. Mind as law brings your thoughts into form.

Form, or effect, is the third aspect of the threefold nature of reality, or of the universal allness. Form or effect is body. It is manifestation. It is the result of a cause set into motion through the law of Mind.

Spirit, law, form—all are contained within the universal allness. It is all one reality, a complete whole and oneness.

So a new idea sets into motion a new creative cause, and you then experience a new effect. The greater your realization of the wholeness of Spirit in, as, and through you and everything in your life, and the more fully you allow this realization to replace any belief in lack or limitation, the more that the wholeness of Spirit expresses in your life. Creative Mind responds to the new beliefs you present to it, producing a like effect in your experience.

The Science of Mind approach for the realization and expression of Spirit in, as, and through you and your life experience is called *spiritual mind treatment*.

What Is Spiritual Mind Treatment?

Spiritual mind treatment is a phrase coined by Ernest Holmes, and it simply means bringing your thinking into alignment with what is true about you as an expression or individualization of Spirit.

Spiritual mind treatment is a way to change your mind about appearances so you begin to see Spirit, or God, in place of a perceived problem or limitation. A powerful method for healing problems and bringing forth a greater good into your life experience, spiritual mind treatment is a way of realizing the presence of Spirit in your life experience and of more fully allowing Spirit to be expressed as and through you.

Traditional prayer reaches *toward* God, addressing God as if God were distant from and apart from the person praying. Spiritual mind treatment differs from traditional prayer in that it involves an awareness of your unity with God, or Spirit, and in this way allows the qualities of Spirit to be more fully expressed in your life.

In spiritual mind treatment the realization that a desired good already is, already exists within you, replaces any belief in limitation. This realization that the good you desire already exists within you establishes a receptivity to the expression of Spirit in, as, and through your life, in whatever specific way you are affirming. Your new belief takes outer form through the operation of creative Mind, or law.

The more you conform your own mind with the wholeness of Spirit, aligning your thinking with the truth, the more you experience wholeness in your life.

How is this done?

Spiritual mind treatment consists of a five-step process. The steps of this process are *recognition, unification, realization, thanksgiving*, and *release*. In the recognition step, you recognize Spirit as being all that exists and everywhere present. In the unification step, you become consciously aware of your oneness with Spirit. In the realization step, you realize the specific way in which Spirit in, as, and through you is expressing in a particular situation or circumstance in your life. In the thanksgiving step, you accept with gratitude that Spirit is expressing in your life in this way. And in the release step, you allow your spiritual mind treatment to set into motion a new cause which is acted upon by law to produce a new effect. (See pages 17-25 for a more detailed explanation of the steps of spiritual mind treatment.)

The key to gaining the most benefit from *It* Is *About You* is to open your mind to the good that is available for you. Become willing to release limiting patterns of thinking. Allow yourself to enter into an awareness of Spirit's presence and power in your life. Have an attitude of expectancy. Cultivate a deep sense of your true nature as Spirit. Apply the ideas and techniques provided in *It* Is *About You*. When you do so, you are sure to see a difference in your life.

The following spiritual mind treatment supports you in benefiting from the ideas and tools presented in this workbook.

Recognition: There is one infinite intelligence and power. Everywhere present, it is always available and constantly active. Whole and complete, it creates all, moves through all, and is the source of all.

Unification: I know that there is nothing separate or apart from this one wholeness. I am an expression of it. It is my true essence. I know that Spirit lives and expresses in, as, and through me, now and always.

Realization: In this deep conviction I realize that success, understanding, and positive accomplishment are the truth of my life. I let go of all belief in limitation or inability. I release everything in my thinking that stands in the way of my success in making positive changes in my life. All doubt falls away. I feel inspired and excited. I have complete faith in Spirit's expression in, as, and through me, and I expect wonderful results as I learn to use spiritual mind treatment to heal my life. I feel loved and supported in this endeavor. Realizing that every form of difficulty is the result of my seeing only in part, I now see perfect wholeness in and as all. The unlimited presence of Spirit expresses in my life now as wonderful new good.

Thanksgiving: Opening to an ever-expanding good in my life, I joyfully give thanks for all that I am experiencing and accomplishing. I am so grateful for my wonderful success.

Release: I now release this spiritual treatment into the creative power of Mind, knowing that the new cause now set in motion returns to me fulfilled perfectly. I allow the activity of Mind to create my new experience of life, and so it does. It is done.

As you read this spiritual mind treatment, you may feel a shift in your attitude—a feeling of greater freedom, lightness, and power. There may be a sense of peace, a release of heaviness or stress. You may experience an energy and expectancy of good. These are evidences of the healing impact of spiritual mind treatment. Now...

Taking Action

...It is time to get started! Here is how to use this book:

Read more about the five steps of spiritual mind treatment on pages 17-25.

Choose the life area you want to start with. The twelve life areas presented are: Health, Finances, Employment, Marriage and Partnership, Children, Parents, Friendship, Emotional Well-Being, Addiction, Life Direction, Aging, and Death and Dying.

Contemplate the quotations from Ernest Holmes and other spiritual teachers included in the introduction to each life area section. Let their words open you to new ways of thinking about your experience in this life area.

Circle the issues that apply to you on the page titled Clarifying the Issue.

On The Truth About You page, determine the purpose of the spiritual mind treatment you are going to write.

Identify the spiritual qualities you desire to realize through your spiritual mind treatment. Turn to page 14 for a list of spiritual qualities.

Use the space provided in this workbook to write your spiritual mind treatment. Here you develop your own personal spiritual mind treatment to resolve the particular problem you have chosen to address. By focusing your attention on the spiritual qualities that are the truth about you and your experience, you establish a new cause which produces a new effect in your life. The creative power of Mind acts on your new belief to bring forth the good you desire.

Continue this process with any other life area you wish to address.

Writing your spiritual mind treatments is the beginning of positive change in your life. Read them often as a way to support this change. Expect results!

"The great adventure lies ahead of you. Discover within yourself that spark of Spirit which may be fanned into a glowing flame, giving you warmth and security. The light from it can certainly and surely guide you to the greatest experience any person can have—the experience of the Universal Presence to whom and through whose Law all things all possible."
—Ernest Holmes

CONCEIVE IT TO ACHIEVE IT

"Whatever you have an equivalent of in your total thought content will become your experience. That is only another way of saying that it is done unto you as you believe."
— Ernest Holmes

Spiritual mind treatment is for the purpose of clearing your thought of beliefs that are limiting or negative. The reason for doing this is to set a new cause into motion. When you clear your thinking of limiting or negative beliefs, and replace them with an awareness of your true nature as Spirit, you attract new conditions into your life. These new conditions reflect your new thinking. Identifying with the qualities of Spirit, you express these qualities in your experience.

Journaling as Preparation for Spiritual Mind Treatment

Journaling is valuable preparation for doing spiritual mind treatment. Writing down your thoughts, feelings, memories, and beliefs about a particular issue in your life helps you to uncover limiting beliefs and also to clarify the specific outcome you desire to realize through spiritual mind treatment.

For example, your journaling may reveal that what you thought was a problem finding a job actually turns out to be a desire for more meaning and direction in your life. Or it may be that a concern about finances deals more directly with fears you have about not being able to care for your aging parents.

The greater clarity you are able to achieve, the more focused and specific you can make your spiritual mind treatment and the more effective it will be.

Journaling is also helpful to you in uncovering attitudes and beliefs that are not producing for you the life experiences you want. Through the process of writing down your feelings, beliefs, and thoughts about an area of your life, you bring up things that lie just beneath the level of your everyday conscious thinking. Even though you may not be aware of these thoughts or beliefs, they nevertheless affect your life experience.

In these ways journaling enhances your ability to achieve a greater good. Only when you can conceive a greater good can you achieve it. The universe can give you only what you take. By clearing away confusion and limiting beliefs, journaling can expand your capacity to receive.

With this in mind, let your journal writing be a free flow of your thoughts and feelings. Give yourself permission to explore your past experiences freely.

Delve honestly into your beliefs and attitudes, your fears and concerns. By bringing them forward in your journal, you gain awareness of issues in your life where healing is needed.

Trust the process. Know that you are now embarking upon a healing journey. The spiritual mind treatments you are writing in this workbook lift you from fear and lack into the truth of your wholeness.

Ask Yourself

Here are some suggested questions to prompt you in your journaling. These questions can apply to all of the life areas.

What am I feeling?
What past experience or memory is related to what I'm feeling?
Is there an underlying fear that I have not faced?
Am I satisfied with this area of my life?
What do I really want to be experiencing?
Do I believe it's possible for me to have what I want?
Do I feel I am worthy of having what I want?
What is in the way of my success and happiness in this area?
Can I imagine a better experience for myself?
What do I want to be feeling?
What do I need to change in my thinking in order to have what I want?
Am I willing to change?

Sample Journal Entries

To assist you in getting started, three sample journal entries are provided here to show how journaling reveals limiting beliefs and attitudes. Journaling can bring into your awareness the cause behind a particular problem area.

Money: Money is scarce. There's never enough. You have to work hard for it and then you don't get paid what you're worth. It's not fair. Other people have lots of money. They must be smarter or luckier than I am. I wonder if I feel worthy enough to have money. Maybe I unconsciously keep myself from having money because I dislike people with money. I must be envious of them. But they have probably worked hard for it. I really do have the money that I need. I'm just not seeing money as a good thing in my life. I'm always feeling fearful about it. My real problem is not so much lack of money as it is a sense of anxiety about my security. I'm afraid I'll end up broke someday. My father had a hard time holding a job. Maybe I'm just expecting the same thing to happen to me. But I have a good job and I'm successful at it. What I really need is not more money but more faith in myself to provide financially for myself and my family.

Addiction: Drinking is not such a bad thing, is it? Everyone drinks. It's the normal way of life. I guess I do drink a lot, though. Why shouldn't I? I'm not hurting anyone. I always make it to work the next day. Maybe I don't feel the best, but I show up. I sometimes have to grab a drink at lunch to get me through the rest of the day, and I don't feel really good about that. There's just such a lot going on in my life, though. If I don't drink, I feel stressed. The drinking is just a way to relax. I need the relief it gives me. When I drink, I don't think about things very much. But if I don't drink, it all comes back to me. I get anxious in the pit of my stomach. I feel lonely, too. I guess I would rather not have to drink but I'm not sure I can stop. Or I don't really want to. I just want to feel okay about myself. I don't feel good enough and that bothers me. That's why I drink. Not because it's fun but because I don't like myself. What I need is to learn to accept who I am and not run away from my feelings. I need to get to know myself. Maybe I'll find out that I really am okay.

Aging: I'm afraid of being useless. It feels like I have nothing going on in my life. It's scary to get old and not have as much energy as I used to have. What's happening to me? I don't know who I am anymore without a job to give my life purpose. People ignore me. It's as if you don't matter unless you're young and have a lot of involvements. I don't have enough to do. That's why I feel so old. It's like being used up, no good anymore. I'm afraid of losing even what friends and activities I still have. There's too much change going on. I want my life to be the way it used to be. I guess I'm living in the past. That's all that seems to have meaning to me. I haven't really thought about getting involved in new activities. I assumed all of that was over for me. And it scares me to start anything new now. What if I'm not good at it? What if no one really wants me? But I could at least try. I think I have to try to re-create myself. There are things I'd like to do. I just need to trust life more.

Identify a Specific Purpose

Through journaling you are guided to a clear understanding of the specific problem or need you are experiencing. Spend some time reading and reflecting on what you have written. Add to it if something else comes to mind. Then when you are ready to do so, identify the specific issue or problem you wish to address.

For example, in the entries given above, the specific issues that come up might be identified as a lack of self-confidence (in the entry about Money), feelings of unworthiness (in the entry about Addiction), and a fear of failure and rejection (in the entry about Aging). Clarifying your underlying issue in this way enables you to do effective spiritual mind treatment, so do take time to feel you have determined the specific purpose you wish to address.

Once you have done so, write down the purpose of your spiritual mind treatment and then state your desired outcome. For example, the purpose of your spiritual mind treatment may be to deal with a concern about weight gain, and your desired outcome would be the willingness to commit to and follow through with healthy eating habits and an exercise routine. You may find as you do spiritual mind treatment for this outcome that you uncover emotional or physical conditions that need to be cleared.

The questionnaires in each life area provide additional help to you in identifying the specific issue which you wish to address through spiritual mind treatment.

Identify Spiritual Qualities

When you explore the problem areas in your life through journaling, you begin to see where your thoughts, feelings, and beliefs are setting up a barrier to greater good in these particular areas. This information is valuable to you in doing spiritual mind treatment, because you are now able to identify a specific purpose for your spiritual mind treatment.

When you do spiritual mind treatment, you are presenting a new cause to creative Mind, which receives the pattern of your thought and then gives physical form to it. The good you realize is established in Mind as a new pattern and it expresses in your experience.

The key to experiencing the good you desire is spiritual awareness. Through your recognition of Spirit in, as, and through you, you provide a clear direction to the creative medium of Mind and thereby open the way for the all-good of Spirit to express more fully in your life. You open yourself to being a clear channel through which the qualities of Spirit can express. These spiritual qualities are an integral part of you. Your true nature is love, wisdom, peace, intelligence, beauty, creativity, and joy.

In his book *How to Use the Science of Mind*, Ernest Holmes gives an example of a man whose life has been consumed with resentment and jealousy. This man has lost all of his friends. He is alone and isolated. He senses that if he can explore deeply enough within himself he can find where the trouble lies and correct it. He begins to look carefully at his thoughts and feelings. He perseveres until he gradually reverses them from resentment and jealousy to a sense of harmony with others. He sees the good in all people. He turns completely away from anything other than the good. The love, always present within him but not allowed to express, now comes forth freely. He attracts many friends.

This story illustrates the healing effect of becoming aware of your oneness with the qualities of Spirit. These qualities are always present within you. Allow them to express. As you conceive, so you achieve.

Spiritual Qualities in and as You

On the following page is a list of many qualities of Spirit. Use this list as an aid in determining the spiritual qualities that you are realizing in your spiritual mind treatment. For example, if your need is for the successful completion of a project at work, the qualities of success, guidance, ease, and confidence may be among the ones you want to realize. Or if your need is to find a relationship partner, you may choose to realize the qualities of love, harmony, enjoyment, and companionship. The need to find care for an aging parent is addressed by such qualities as comfort, gentleness, caring, and compassion. In the case of a back injury you may choose to realize wholeness, ease, strength, and support.

Identify the qualities of Spirit you desire to experience in the situation or condition for which you are doing spiritual mind treatment. Then in the recognition step of your treatment, acknowledge the presence of these qualities in and as that situation or condition. In the unification step, become consciously aware of your unity with these qualities. Accept that they are the truth of who you are.

With this acceptance in mind, go on in the realization step of your spiritual mind treatment to realize that these qualities are right now established in and as the particular situation or condition. In this way, you are setting into motion a new cause. The new cause brings about a new experience.

Next, the thanksgiving step reinforces in your mind the new thought that the spiritual qualities you have identified as true about you are true, further deepening your acceptance of them. Finally, the release step activates the creative power of Mind to bring forth what you realize to be true.

By continuing to focus your thoughts on these spiritual qualities as the truth of you and your life, you cultivate their expression in your life.

Ability	Abundance	Acceptance
Agility	Assurance	Authenticity
Awareness	Balance	Beauty
Boldness	Caring	Cheerfulness
Clarity	Comfort	Commitment
Companionship	Compassion	Competence
Confidence	Contentment	Cooperation
Courage	Creativity	Determination
Direction	Discernment	Ease
Empathy	Energy	Enjoyment
Enthusiasm	Equanimity	Expansion
Fairness	Faith	Fidelity
Forgiveness	Freedom	Friendliness
Fulfillment	Generosity	Gentleness
Givingness	Goodness	Grace
Growth	Guidance	Happiness
Harmony	Health	Honesty
Illumination	Inspiration	Integrity
Intelligence	Joy	Justice
Kindness	Knowledge	Love
Loyalty	Mastery	Meaning
Oneness	Openness	Opportunity
Order	Passion	Patience
Peace	Perfection	Perseverance
Poise	Power	Prosperity
Protection	Purity	Purpose
Reconciliation	Recovery	Renewal
Resolve	Right Action	Serenity
Silence	Stability	Stillness
Strength	Success	Supply
Support	Tenacity	Tenderness
Timeliness	Transcendence	Trustworthiness
Truth	Understanding	Unity
Vigor	Vitality	Well-being
Wholeness	Wisdom	Worth
Zeal		

A Spiritual Mind Treatment for New Beliefs

Outcome of treatment: My thinking is cleared of limiting beliefs and I embrace new beliefs that align with the truth of my spiritual nature.

Recognition: I recognize the presence of Spirit everywhere in the universe, in, as, and through all that exists. The invisible essence of everything and the infinite source of all, Spirit expresses in the world as clarity, understanding, and freedom.

Unification: Knowing that nothing is opposed to or separate from Spirit, I enter deeply into an awareness of my unity with Spirit. I know that I am one with the qualities of clarity, understanding, and freedom which are the truth of Spirit and that these qualities live and express in, as, and through me, now and always.

Realization: In this deep conviction, I declare that my thoughts, feelings, and beliefs are all in harmony with the perfection of Spirit. I am free of all confusion and negativity, for I know that the understanding, clarity, and freedom of Spirit live in and as me. I understand my true nature as an expression of Spirit, and I choose right now to express this true nature. I allow Spirit to express fully in and as me in every way. My thoughts, feelings, and beliefs align perfectly with the wholeness and perfection of Spirit. Nothing can limit my effective use of spiritual mind treatment, for I know the truth of who I am. I release anything in my conscious and subconscious mind that is not the truth, and I realize the truth right now. How joyous it is to open to the free flow of Spirit in and through my life!

Thanksgiving: Opening myself to an ever-expanding good, I allow Spirit to express in my life as clarity, understanding, and freedom. I give thanks as I joyously receive this good. I am grateful.

Release: Releasing this word into the creative activity of Mind, I am confident that my thoughts are cleared of all that is unlike Spirit. So I simply allow the creative power of the universe to bring forth a new experience in my life of spiritual understanding, clarity, and freedom. It is done, and so it is.

Healing Your Life
The Five Steps of Spiritual Mind
Treatment

In order to prepare a meaningful spiritual mind treatment, you'll need to have a good understanding of the purpose of each step. As mentioned before, the five steps are: recognition, unification, realization, thanksgiving, and release. Here they are discussed in more depth.

Recognition

Recognition is the first step of spiritual mind treatment. In this step you recognize Spirit as absolute being, the one source of all that exists. Spirit is the wholeness and perfection that is the true nature of everything. It is the first cause of all form.

Purpose of the recognition step of spiritual mind treatment:
To create within yourself a deep consciousness of the presence of Spirit in, as, and through all, as the ultimate source and true nature of all.

Suggestions for writing an effective statement of recognition:
A recognition statement reflects the depth of your conviction that there is a spiritual presence and power in the universe. In preparing to write your statement, become quiet and contemplate the nature of Spirit. You may wish to use other words for Spirit, such as life, the all-good, or infinite intelligence. It doesn't matter what word you use; what matters is your deep sense of a presence and power, eternal and abiding.

Consider the qualities of Spirit—love, peace, joy, wisdom, abundance, beauty. Think about the meaning of these qualities for you. Refer to the list on page 14 for other qualities. Choose those that answer the particular need for which you are doing spiritual mind treatment. Contemplate Spirit as these qualities until you reach a deep level of recognition of Spirit in expression as these qualities.

Then put words to your thoughts, journaling if you feel moved to do so, and write a statement of what you recognize about Spirit. Record your statement on the appropriate page in this workbook.

Examples of recognition statements:

I know there is a presence and power in the universe that is the source of all life. This presence is Spirit. It is the perfect wholeness that is the true essence of all that exists. I sense Spirit in the outer world as love, as beauty, as harmony. I know Spirit lives in and permeates all.

There is one life, one absolute being in and through all. This life is perfect and it is the life of God, of Spirit. It is the source of all good and I recognize this source right now in and as everything around me. I see it in the infinite skies and in the continual renewal of nature. It is the limitless source of all good things, always present, always available.

I recognize the infinite intelligence of the universe. It is the Mind that is behind all that exists. It is the source of all, and is in and through all things. There is nothing separate from it and nothing that can limit its perfect action. It always knows what to do, how to do it, and when to do it. It is the source of every good thing. I see it expressing as balance, order, and right guidance.

Unification

Unification is the second step of spiritual mind treatment. In this step, after you have recognized Spirit as the ultimate source of all that exists, you become consciously aware of your unity with Spirit. You accept that Spirit is your true essence and affirm that you express its creative power through your thought.

Purpose of the unification step of spiritual mind treatment:
To know and understand that because Spirit, which is whole and perfect, is the true essence of all that exists and is the truth about you. In this step you become aware that you are a unique individualized expression of the one source and its life is your life now.

Suggestions for creating an effective statement of unification:
In your statement of unification, acknowledge your oneness with Spirit. Consciously sense and feel the presence and power of Spirit within you and also as you. Know that because Spirit is all there is, you are part of Spirit.

Let go of any feeling of separation and fill your mind with a deep sense of your oneness. Relate to the world around you as one with it. In contemplating the idea that Spirit is all there is, consider the qualities of Spirit, such as cooperation, givingness, joy, and compassion. Identify yourself as these qualities. Know that this is your true nature.

When you have sensed your oneness with Spirit as fully as you can, begin to write your statement of unification, letting it come forth with a deep sense of conviction. It may be helpful to journal about your sense of connection with all of life as a way to further deepen this conviction. When you are ready, record your statement on the appropriate page of this workbook.

Examples of unification statements:
I know I am one with Spirit. Spirit is within me and guides me at all times. I accept this unity completely and I experience the flow of the divine nature in and through me.

Deeply aware of the infinite presence that lives within me, I let go of any sense of separation and joyfully embrace my oneness with all that is. Whatever is true of it is also true of me. I know and accept that I am one with the all-good.

There is one life, that life is God, that life is perfect, and that life is my life now. There is nothing in me or in my experience separate from God. My mind is a focal point, an individualized center, in the Mind of God, the one creative power. I open myself to the free expression of perfect life through me.

Realization

Realization is the third step of spiritual mind treatment. When you come to this step, you are consciously aware of the presence of Spirit in, as, and through all, and of your oneness with Spirit as your true nature. You are now realizing, without any doubt or reservation, that the good you desire to experience in your life is already established in Spirit, in universal Mind.

Purpose of the realization step of spiritual mind treatment:
A realization statement sets into motion a new cause which takes form in your experience. The new cause is realized through the action of a universal creative power, which your thought directs. Make your statement as clear and specific as possible. In your statement declare what you want to experience. Be positive and convinced that you have the good you desire. Affirm that the good you want is already yours right now. See the result happening. See and feel yourself experiencing this good and accept it.

When you are ready to write your realization statement, do so with enthusiasm and feeling. Put energy into it. Know that you are now directing the creative power of Mind, which responds to your realization according to your conviction and acceptance. Be definite. Allow your imagination to really see and feel the good as yours now. Then write your statement on the appropriate page in this workbook.

Examples of realization statements:
For money: Money is in infinite supply. Money flows freely to me, enabling me to be comfortable and prosperous. I have the money I need to enjoy life and to give generously. Life withholds no good from me. Money is a form of the infinite abundance of the universe, and I accept this abundance in my life now. I see myself as secure, comfortable, and affluent. I attract money easily and all I need is mine now.

For employment: I now have the perfect job. I have employment that is totally right for me. I love my work. I engage in it enthusiastically and productively. I enjoy what I do and the people I work with. I am paid well for the work I do. It is fulfilling and worthwhile. My job has the hours and benefits that I desire, and the location of it is convenient. In this job I am able to express my abilities fully.

For health: My body is a physical expression of infinite life. I affirm that the activity of every function and organ of my body is harmonious. I accept perfect wholeness as the truth of my body. The one perfect life in me, as me, is maintaining every atom and cell of my body. I feel wonderful! I breathe, sleep, and move with total ease. I now experience the ever-available energy, power, and vitality of Spirit, flowing feely through me.

Thanksgiving

Thanksgiving is the fourth step of spiritual mind treatment. In this step, you thankfully accept the good that you are realizing as your experience now. You express your gratitude for it, allowing a deep sense of its realization to permeate your thought.

Purpose of the thanksgiving step of spiritual mind treatment:
To deepen your acceptance of the desired good as true of your life right now. When gratitude is expressed, the thought and feeling of having already received is impressed in the mind. This strong sense of acceptance is a key element in spiritual mind treatment. When you accept something, you know it is yours and you act accordingly.

Suggestions for writing an effective statement of thanksgiving:
A statement of thanksgiving expresses how you feel about receiving the good you have directed universal Mind to create in your life. Be convinced that you have it now. Let go of any sense that it may not be possible or that you may not be worthy of it.

Create a statement of thanksgiving that conveys your appreciation for the way Spirit within you is expressing in your life. In this way you open yourself to a deeper acceptance of and receptivity to the all-good.

Let your heart be filled with thanksgiving that you are now experiencing what you desire. Then write the words that come from this feeling of gratitude. Enjoy the sense of knowing that something wonderful has been accomplished. Record your statement on the appropriate page of this workbook.

Examples of thanksgiving statements:
With joy I now acknowledge and accept the perfect fulfillment of my desired good. That which I am realizing is absolutely assured. I know with complete conviction that it is established in my life already, and I gratefully affirm and accept for myself the love, abundance, and givingness of God now and always. Joyously I give thanks for the healing and renewal I now experience. I am so deeply grateful for the wholeness and perfection of Spirit expressing in and as my life, now and always. Thank you, God.

I accept with heartfelt gratitude the creative action of the words I have spoken. I believe with total certainty that the unfailing power of Spirit is at this very moment drawing my good to me, and I rest in an attitude of deep thanksgiving. Freely and gratefully I accept the good now appearing in my life. I am so deeply grateful for this wonderful new experience manifesting right here and right now, and I say thank you.

What a strong sense of thanksgiving and faith I feel! I have perfect faith in the infinite creative power of life to fulfill my word. With praise and thanksgiving, I bless the spiritual reality behind all things and accept it as my truth. The good I seek now comes forth into my experience, and I joyously open my heart and mind to receive it. I accept my good with deep gratitude, knowing that all is well. I am truly grateful.

Release

Release is the fifth step of spiritual mind treatment. In this step, you are completing your spiritual mind treatment by releasing it to the creative activity of Mind. You acknowledge that a new cause is now established in the mental world and can sustain itself without any further action by you. You are free of any and all concern regarding the fulfillment of the cause you have set into motion. It is fulfilled. You know this and are completely convinced that your spiritual mind treatment is already producing results.

Purpose of the release step of spiritual mind treatment:
To mentally and emotionally let go of your spiritual mind treatment and allow the creative power of Mind to fulfill it in your life experience. You emphasize in this way the total acceptance of your desired good. You are now free to act as though the good you desire is already accomplished and is present in your life. There is a total release and trust. It is done.

Suggestions for writing an effective statement of release:
In a statement of release, you completely let go of both your spiritual mind treatment and your concern about the problem you are addressing. When you have completed your spiritual mind treatment, take your thoughts away from the issue and focus instead on the good you desire as already established. Let go and trust the perfect activity of Mind. Make your release statement strong and certain, leaving you with the conviction that you have entirely let go of your spiritual mind treatment and are now experiencing its result. Relax and know that you do not have to do anything further. Your work is done.

When you have reached a strong feeling of release in your mind and completely accept the truth of your realization, write a definite statement of release. Record your statement on the appropriate page of this workbook.

Examples of release statements:
Knowing that the creative power of Mind is now responding to the new cause set into motion, I release all concern for the outcome. I am at peace. I let go and accept. It is done. And so it is.

I joyfully release this spiritual mind treatment into the unfailing action of law, accepting the new expression of Spirit in my experience. I know that Mind is already creating for me the good I desire. It is done. And so it is.

I know and accept that the perfect activity of universal Law is bringing forth right now the good I have established in Mind. I release this spiritual mind treatment with complete confidence and faith. I know it is done. And so it is.

PART TWO
Using the
Power for Good

Spiritual Mind Treatment

"There is a power for good in the universe and you can use it."

—Ernest Holmes

In this section you are writing your own spiritual mind treatments, using what you have learned in Part One of this workbook. Start with any of the twelve life areas and work through all of them in any order you wish. Each life area section consists of:

- A quotation from Ernest Holmes pertaining to the life area
- A brief commentary on the life area
- Ideas for contemplation from contemporary spiritual teachers
- Clarifying the issue
- The truth about you
- Writing the five steps of your spiritual mind treatment
- Your completed spiritual mind treatment
- An example of a spiritual mind treatment for that life area

How to Work with the Life Area Sections

(1) After choosing the life area you want to begin with, read the introductory material for insight into any changes you wish to experience in this life area and complete the two self-assessment portions of the chapter (Ideas for Contemplation and Clarifying the Issue). The result of your work with these pages will guide you in determining the particular issue in this life area you want to do spiritual mind treatment for.

(2) Now that you know the particular issue you wish to address, turn in the appropriate life area to the page titled The Truth About You. Write down the desired outcome for your spiritual mind treatment at the bottom of the page. Be as specific as you can. Some examples are: "I am free of back pain." "There is harmony in my relationship with my parents." "I have work that uses my gifts and abilities and that pays enough for me to live comfortably." "I forgive and release the past, and I am at peace with myself." "I am living in my ideal home."

(3) Use the next five pages for developing your expression of your spiritual mind

treatment: recognition, unification, realization, thanksgiving, and release. Be sure to keep all of your statements in the present tense: "I am free of back pain," not "I will be free of back pain." Journaling can help you deepen the felt sense you have of the truth of what you are writing in your recognition and unification steps.

(4) When you come to the realization step, refer to the outcome realized at the bottom of page entitled The Truth About Me for guidance in stating the realization step of your spiritual mind treatment. Use this statement as a starting point, adding as many specific details as come to mind. What is your new experience like? If it is a new job you are realizing for yourself, for example, include statements that tell about your new office, your clients, the pay you're receiving, the colleagues you enjoy working with—anything that makes the experience real for you. Also include statements about how the new experience feels. Are you are excited, joyous, free, energized, peaceful? Express how the new experience that you are realizing feels to you. It is a combination of feeling and words that produces the desired result. Include statements about the spiritual qualities you are realizing. Be specific and clear.

(5) Turn now to the page titled My Spiritual Mind Treatment and record the key statements from the previous five pages—the statements that have special power for you. This is your spiritual mind treatment.

(6) For guidance in writing your spiritual mind treatment, see the sample spiritual mind treatment dealing with a particular issue in each life area. Also you may wish to review the explanation of the five steps of spiritual mind treatment on pages 17-25 as you move throughout this process.

Your Follow-Up Actions

Where do you go from here? By writing your spiritual mind treatment, you have started a process of healing and renewal in your life. Positive results are already happening. Here are some things you can do to support the process of positive change:

• Be alert to the way you think about the condition for which you are doing spiritual mind treatment. Stay in an attitude of positive expectancy regarding the outcome.

- Read your spiritual mind treatment several times each day. Recommended times to do this are when you first wake up in the morning and before you go to bed in the evening. Read your spiritual mind treatment out loud. Take time to contemplate it. Experience the feelings associated with each of the five steps. If any of your statements seems to lose impact for you, rewrite it.

- Follow any inner guidance that comes to you. Spirit works in your life through inner guidance, which may come as a gentle nudge, a sense of inspiration, or a flash of insight. You may feel a kind of "pull" to do a particular action. Remain open to this guidance and respond to it.

- Give the process the time it takes. There is a natural unfolding of events. Allow this unfolding to occur. It may take days or months or it may happen right away. Keep deepening your conviction as you continue working with your spiritual mind treatment. Make it a vital, real truth in your life. When you do so, the outcome is assured.

How Is Your Life Changing?

Things happen as a result of spiritual mind treatment, because a new cause is acted upon by universal law. Through your spiritual mind treatment, you are replacing a limiting thought—for example, that back pain is something you just have to live with—with a realization of the truth about you—that you are one with the support, wholeness, and perfect functioning of Spirit.

You are presenting a new cause to universal law, which automatically creates an effect in accordance with the cause presented.

Now it is time for you to be alert to changes in your life experience. Writing about these changes helps to support the natural unfolding in your life of healing and renewal. Use a separate journal for this record. Here are some questions to address in your journal:

- What changes are you experiencing in your life as a result of doing your spiritual mind treatment? Include those changes that may not seem to be related to your particular issue but that are positive developments for you. Also consider changes not only in physical form but also in your attitudes and beliefs.
- Do you have any new realizations regarding this issue?
- What actions have you felt guided to take?
- What is your understanding about Spirit now?
- Has your awareness of who you are, of your true nature, changed? If so, in

what way?
- After doing spiritual mind treatment for an issue relating to one life area, are other areas of your life beginning to flow more easily?

Select one of the twelve life areas and begin to create your spiritual mind treatment. Let the power for good change your life for the better.

PART THREE
Life Areas
Workbook

HEALTH

"Health and sickness are largely externalizations of our dominant mental and spiritual states. .... Worry, fear, anger, jealousy, and other emotional conditions, are mental in their nature, and as such are being recognized as the hidden cause of a large part of physical suffering. A normal healthy mind reflects itself in a healthy body, and conversely, an abnormal mental state expresses its corresponding condition in some physical condition."

—Ernest Holmes

The word *health* means wholeness. Wholeness is your true, natural state. The full expression of your wholeness depends on your inner acceptance and awareness of it—on your thoughts, feelings, beliefs, and attitudes. As Ernest Holmes has said, "To the extent we know that God as Life is perfect, whole, and complete; to the extent we can mentally accept the Perfection of the One Life as our life, then to that extent will we be able to enjoy and experience health."

When you accept the qualities of Spirit as true about you, then these qualities become outwardly realized and expressed in your life. You experience health. So health begins in the mind. Your mind is a creative center for the activity of universal Mind.

If the main focus of your thinking is on vitality, wholeness, and physical well-being, you are directing Mind to create for you a healthy body and you experience the normal functioning of your physical body. But if you focus on illness, impairment, or disease, then you attract to yourself some form of illness, impairment, or disease. In back of every physical disturbance there is some mental cause.

You can change this cause by identifying and letting go of beliefs that negate your true, natural state of wholeness. The questionnaire and positive statements that follow will help you to discover any negativity in your thought patterns and to re-focus your thinking in a positive, health-producing direction. As you open to ideas of vitality, energy, wholeness, perfection, power, or any of the other spiritual qualities that evoke a strong mental or emotional response within you, you will re-form your physical state in accordance with those new ideas.

Affirm for yourself a body that is spiritually whole and perfect, that is functioning fully and harmoniously. The spiritual reality is present, here and now. The outer form always corresponds with the inner form, or idea, held in mind. So as you align with the perfection of Spirit, you bring into outer form that physical perfection which is your true nature.

Know that as a center in the wholeness and perfection of Spirit, you already

35

possess the gift of radiant good health. It always exists in potential, and through aligning your thinking with it you bring it forth. You can choose to be healthy. Spiritual mind treatment is a tool by which you realize in your mind, and then demonstrate in your life experience, the spiritual truth of health.

Ideas for Contemplation

"Since Spirit is all there is, the different areas of our experience are points along a continuum, not distinct and separate aspects of our being. The emotions are Spirit in disguise and the physical body is also Spirit in disguise. So if there is healing in the body, there will be healing in all other areas. One will affect the others."

—Deepak Chopra

"Negative emotions that are not faced, accepted, and then let go, leave a residue of emotional pain, which is stored in the cells of the body."

—Eckhart Tolle

"Every thought you think and every word you speak is affirming something. It could be affirming negative stuff or it could be affirming positive stuff. Every thought is creating something in your life."

—Louise Hay

Contemplate these ideas. How do you feel about them? Do these ideas open you to new ways of thinking? Are you seeing ways in which limiting beliefs have affected your experience? Record below any new awareness or insights regarding your beliefs in the life area of Health:

Clarifying the Issue

You have become aware of limiting beliefs and are opening to new ways of think-ing about your experience in the life area of Health. Use this list of statements to clarify the particular issues you want to heal through spiritual mind treatment. Circle the issues that apply to you. Write at the bottom of this page any addition-al issues not listed here.

I'm always catching a cold or the flu.

I have problems with my weight.

My energy level is low.

I have difficulty sleeping.

I'm afraid to have the surgery I need.

I have many allergies.

My sexual functioning is poor.

I often get feelings of dizziness.

I have shortness of breath.

I'm afraid I've inherited family illnesses.

I have frequent headaches.

Arthritis is bothering me.

I have problems with my digestion.

I'm often caught up in fear about getting ill.

I can't stop smoking.

I lack the discipline to exercise.

I have back pain.

Other:

The Truth About You

Behind an experience of limitation is a belief in limitation. You can replace limiting beliefs by affirming the spiritual truth about you. In the list on the right are statements of spiritual truth. Use them as guides in stating the outcome you desire to realize through your spiritual mind treatment. At the bottom of the page, write the outcome you are realizing. Then use the following pages for the five steps of your spiritual mind treatment. An example of a spiritual mind treatment in the life area of Health is found on page 46.

If you have been saying:	*Now begin to say:*
I always get the flu.	I am well and healthy.
I can't control my weight.	I maintain my ideal weight easily.
I don't have any energy.	I am vital and energetic.
I can't sleep at night.	I sleep deeply all night long.
I'm afraid I won't recover from surgery.	I recover completely from surgery.
I'm afraid of heart trouble.	I have a strong heart.
I suffer from a lot of allergies.	I am clear of all allergies.
I'm in constant pain.	I am free from pain.
I have a bad back.	My back is strong and flexible.
I don't heal quickly.	I heal easily and quickly.
Everyone in my family gets ulcers.	I am healthy and free of stress.
Arthritis is hindering my movement.	My body moves with ease.
High blood pressure runs in my family.	My blood pressure is normal.
I've never been very healthy.	I enjoy excellent health.
I'm afraid of getting cancer.	I am safe and free of all fear.

Record here the outcome you are realizing through your spiritual mind treatment:

Developing Your Spiritual Mind Treatment for Health

The following five pages are for your use in journaling about each step of your spiritual mind treatment and for exploring the language that is most meaningful to you. After you've done so, you will write your spiritual mind treatment on the page provided.

Recognition

Spirit is the essence of all that exists. Notice evidence of the presence of Spirit around you. Which spiritual qualities express the truth about your experience in the life area of Health? Recognize the presence of these qualities in your recognition step. Write your statement of recognition here, making it as sincere and meaningful as you can. See pages 17-18 for an explanation of this step of spiritual mind treatment.

Unification

As you recognize the presence of Spirit all around you, begin now to become aware of your connection with Spirit. Feel your oneness with the qualities of Spirit. Sense these spiritual qualities in, as, and through your life. Write a statement here that expresses your awareness of your unity with Spirit. See page 19 for an explanation of this step of spiritual mind treatment.

Realization

Your statement of realization sets into motion a new cause which you experience as a new effect. By affirming the spiritual truth about you and identifying with the spiritual qualities you wish to express, you establish these qualities in and as your experience. Write your statement of realization here, including details and feelings that make it real and vivid for you. Be clear, definite, and specific. Remember to state your realization positively and to use the present tense. See pages 20-21 for an explanation of this step of spiritual mind treatment.

Thanksgiving

Giving thanks reinforces your sense of having received and accepted something. Here, with deep conviction, express your gratitude that your issue in the life area of Health is now resolved and that your healing is already established. See pages 22-23 for an explanation of this step of spiritual mind treatment.

Release

Releasing your spiritual mind treatment directs the creative power of universal Mind, or law, to fulfill the new cause presented to it. With complete faith in the unfailing power of law, you let it go, knowing that a new cause is set in motion. You know it is done. Write your statement of release here. See pages 24–25 for an explanation of this step of spiritual mind treatment.

Your Spiritual Mind Treatment for Health

Combined together, the statements you have written on the previous five pages comprise your complete spiritual mind treatment for the life area of Health. Review your statements to be sure they evoke a deep feeling and conviction in you. Also make sure that the statements you have written for each of the steps of spiritual mind treatment fulfill the intended purpose of that step. Express the essence of each step of your spiritual mind treatment here.

When you are ready, write your statements here:

Recognition:

Unification:

Realization:

Thanksgiving:

Release:

See pages 30-31 for suggestions on what to do now that you have completed your spiritual mind treatment for the life area of Health.

Example of a Spiritual Mind Treatment for Health

The following spiritual mind treatment is intended as a guide only. The effectiveness of your spiritual mind treatment is enhanced when you use words and statements that have the most meaning for you.

Problem to be addressed: Skin infection
Outcome: Healing of skin infection and overall health and vitality restored

Recognition:
There is one eternal, universal Mind that is everywhere present and that is the source and essence of all that exists. As the changeless Spirit in, as, and through all, it is complete, whole, and perfect.

Unification:
Knowing that Spirit is all that exists and is the source of everything, I am consciously aware right now that my own true nature is the wholeness and perfection of Spirit. I am an individualized center in the Mind of God. There is no separation or division, only oneness. My mind is inseparably connected with the infinite Mind of Spirit, because it is all that exists. I know that I am identical in essence with the wholeness and perfection of Spirit.

Realization:
I now realize that everything about me, including my physical body, is an expression and reflection of the wholeness and perfection of Spirit. There can be no disease of any kind within Spirit. All appearance of disease, in the form of a skin infection, is now eliminated, and all the false beliefs that have given rise to the appearance of disease are now replaced with a deep awareness and conviction of Spirit's wholeness and perfection in and as my body. A perfect cause now manifests in my body as perfect skin. I am free of anything unlike this perfect cause, because it is my true nature. It now expresses fully and freely, and I see only perfect functioning in every cell of my body. My inherent perfection is now revealed. Any anger, resentment, or inner conflict is completely dissolved, and I am at peace. I feel revitalized and refreshed, and there is an infusion of new life and joy within me. God's perfect life is my life now.

Thanksgiving:
Accepting the perfect healing of my physical body, I gratefully allow Spirit to radiate completely as wholeness and perfection in my life. I give thanks for this full and free expression of Spirit in, as, and through all that concerns me.

Release:

I release this word now into the activity of infinite Mind, allowing the creative medium of Mind to bring into manifestation the truth of my wholeness and perfection. Knowing that Mind works infallibly to express in my life the spiritual truth of wholeness and perfection, I let the perfect activity of Mind fulfill this word. It is done. And so it is.

FINANCES

"Success and prosperity are spiritual attributes belonging to all people. This is the key to a realization of a more abundant life, to the demonstration of success in financial matters. It is right that we should be successful, for otherwise Spirit is not expressed."

—Ernest Holmes

Prosperity awaits your recognition and acceptance of it. You are always attracting to you that which you accept. Financial abundance becomes a tangible, physical reality in your life when you open your mind to receive it.

Everywhere present is an unlimited, formless Spirit out of which everything is made. By seeing yourself as abundantly prosperous, you provide a pattern to the universal law that gives form to the limitless substance of Spirit, the source and cause of all. You can always draw on Spirit for any desired good. If you wish greater financial success, give up the idea that money is scarce or hard to acquire and that lack is a "fact of life." Free yourself from these and other limiting beliefs, and replace them with the knowledge that everything you need is available to you in infinite supply. Then turn all of your attention to the acceptance of your good.

When you cultivate a consciousness of wealth, money will be attracted to you. Spirit cannot help but respond to your deeply-held belief and conviction in your abundant prosperity. You may receive a raise at work, an investment may return a large dividend, or a business opportunity may come along. However it comes, money will begin to flow into your life.

Identify yourself with the greater financial supply you desire. Train yourself to think about it with the feeling that it is naturally yours—and that it is already yours. Truly believe and feel with your whole being that financial success and abundance are available to you and are secured right now. Then act as though abundance is already established in your life. Think and appear prosperous. Make financial well-being a real, living part of your everyday experience by consistently believing in it, expecting it and acting daily from an intention to be useful and valuable. Results are assured.

Choose the spiritual qualities that you associate with financial well-being, and become consciously aware that these qualities are your true nature.

Ideas for Contemplation

"To prosper, we must recognize that we are spiritual beings and that through the action of the mind we can make whatever contact we need to make with divine intelligence, directing it in our life in whatever way seems best. We just need to dare to prosper—meaning we dare to accept wholeness and well-being into our life."

—Catherine Ponder

"Spirit is infinite and it's always expressing. We just become bigger and bigger places for it to express through."

—Michael Bernard Beckwith

"We make up stories about ourselves— 'I'm not worthy,' 'I'm not enough,' 'I'm bad.' Most human beings are living to prove one of these stories is true—or not true. We create circumstances to live within or beyond the story."

—Iyanla Vanzant

"My life has been a constant unfolding. Joseph Campbell said, 'Follow your bliss,' and I have. I would pick up and move whenever I sensed there was an opportunity that would allow me to fulfill my potential. I've always given myself permission to do what felt right."

—Jack Canfield

Contemplate these ideas. How do you feel about them? Do these ideas open you to new ways of thinking? Are you seeing ways in which limiting beliefs have affected your experience? Record below any new awareness or insights regarding your beliefs in the life area of Finances:

Clarifying the Issue

You have become aware of limiting beliefs and are opening to new ways of thinking about your experience in the life area of Finances. Use this list of statements to clarify the particular issues you want to heal through spiritual mind treatment. Circle the issues that apply to you. Write at the bottom of this page any additional issues not listed here.

My salary isn't enough to live on.

I spend too much money.

I can't support my family.

I never have enough money.

My credit rating is poor.

I have a problem getting raises.

I can't afford the things my children need.

I can't save money.

I'm facing bankruptcy.

I gamble too much.

I can't pay my bills.

I've made bad investments.

I'm worried about providing for retirement.

I can't afford to buy a home.

My business is failing.

Other:

The Truth About You

Behind an experience of limitation is a belief in limitation. You can replace limiting beliefs by affirming the spiritual truth about you. In the list on the right are statements of spiritual truth. Use them as guides in stating the outcome you desire to realize through your spiritual mind treatment. At the bottom of the page, write the outcome you are realizing. Then use the following pages for the five steps of your spiritual mind treatment. An example of a spiritual mind treatment in the life area of Finances is found on page 59.

If you have been saying:	*Now begin to say:*
I don't earn enough money.	I earn an abundant amount of money.
I spend too much money.	I spend my money wisely.
I have a poor credit rating.	My credit rating is excellent.
I have problems getting raises.	I earn and receive raises easily.
I have difficulty saving money.	I am able to save money, and I do.
I'm facing bankruptcy.	My finances are in sound condition.
I gamble too much.	I am free of any need to gamble.
I can't pay my bills.	All of my bills are paid on time.
I can't afford the things I need.	I have all the money I need.
I'm always worrying about money.	I am safe and cared for in every way.
I can't provide for my retirement.	I have enough money for retirement.
I can't manage my money.	I manage my money well.
I'm afraid of having to do without.	All of my needs are met.
My investments are not doing well.	I receive good investment income.

Record here the outcome you are realizing through your spiritual mind treatment:

Developing Your Spiritual Mind Treatment for Finances

The following five pages are for your use in journaling about each step of your spiritual mind treatment and for exploring the language that is most meaningful to you. After you've done so, you will write your spiritual mind treatment on the page provided.

Recognition

Spirit is the essence of all that exists. Notice evidence of the presence of Spirit around you. Which spiritual qualities express the truth about your experience in the life area of Finances? Recognize the presence of these qualities in your recognition step. Write your statement of recognition here, making it as sincere and meaningful as you can. See pages 17-18 for an explanation of this step of spiritual mind treatment.

Unification

As you recognize the presence of Spirit all around you, begin now to become aware of your connection with Spirit. Feel your oneness with the qualities of Spirit. Sense these spiritual qualities in, as, and through your life. Write a statement here that expresses your awareness of your unity with Spirit. See page 19 for an explanation of this step of spiritual mind treatment.

Realization

Your statement of realization sets into motion a new cause which you experience as a new effect. By affirming the spiritual truth about you, identifying with the spiritual qualities you wish to express, you establish these qualities in and as your experience. Write your statement of realization here, including details and feelings that make it real and vivid for you. Be clear, definite, and specific. Remember to state your realization positively and to use the present tense. See pages 20-21 for an explanation of this step of spiritual mind treatment.

Thanksgiving

Giving thanks reinforces your sense of having received and accepted something. Here, with deep conviction, express your gratitude that your issue in the life area of Finances is now resolved and that your healing is already established. See pages 22-23 for an explanation of this step of spiritual mind treatment.

Release

Releasing your spiritual mind treatment directs the creative power of universal Mind, or law, to fulfill the new cause presented to it. With complete faith in the unfailing power of law, you present your new cause to be realized. You let it go, knowing it is done. Write your statement of release here. See pages 24–25 for an explanation of this step of spiritual mind treatment.

Your Spiritual Mind Treatment for Finances

Combined together, the statements you have written on the previous five pages comprise your complete spiritual mind treatment for the life area of Finances. Review your statements to be sure they evoke a deep feeling and conviction in you. Also make sure that the statements you have written for each of the steps of spiritual mind treatment fulfill the intended purpose of that step. Express the essence of each step of your spiritual mind treatment here.

When you are ready, write your statements here:

Recognition:

Unification:

Realization:

Thanksgiving:

Release:

See pages 30–31 for suggestions on what to do now that you have completed your spiritual mind treatment for the life area of Finances.

Example of a Spiritual Mind Treatment for Finances

The following spiritual mind treatment is intended as a guide only. The effectiveness of your spiritual mind treatment is enhanced when you use words and statements that have the most meaning for you.

Problem to be addressed: Not enough money
Outcome: I have money to meet all of my financial needs

Recognition:
I recognize the presence everywhere of infinite good, a freely giving source of overflowing abundance in the universe. Spirit is limitless. Around and through all, this inexhaustible source expresses as abundance of all kinds, including money and financial prosperity.

Unification:
Knowing that the abundance of good surrounds and permeates all that exists in the universe, I am aware of my oneness with it. The good that exists everywhere expresses and flows within me. I am one with the abundance of the infinite.

Realization:
I realize right now that I experience the abundance of infinite Spirit. I participate fully and freely in the pouring forth of this abundance. It comes to me in the form of money, financial increase, and material prosperity. I have more than ample money for whatever I desire to do and I enjoy life to the fullest. I am abundant in every way. All the money I need flows to me easily and readily. I am completely comfortable with my financial situation and feel no worry whatsoever. I am rich and prosperous. All concerns about my finances are now resolved. I am open and receptive to the generous outpouring of abundance from the infinite good, and I accept it joyously.

Thanksgiving:
Giving grateful praise for the wonderful good now established in my life, I say a heartfelt thank you for the bountiful abundance that is now mine.

Release:
With complete conviction that financial good is manifesting right now, I release this treatment to the perfect action of the law of Mind, knowing it is done. And so it is.

EMPLOYMENT

"Spirit surrounds you and is unlimited, and is the source of all things. This limitless source is merely waiting for you to place your order; so with an attitude of perfect acceptance declare that you are divinely employed and compensated. Without question you have set a law in motion which will produce something good."

—Ernest Holmes

There is a right and perfect position for you. Nothing can hinder the creative activity of universal Mind in and through you, and all necessary channels open up for this activity to express in your life as the ideal job or employment for you. Your essential nature is Spirit. You are in partnership with the infinite. Know that this partnership always leads to success. Spirit is always manifesting itself and it does so now through the thought pattern that you establish for yourself.

You are part of Spirit and the essential nature of Spirit is always perfect and always active. There is a presence and a power immediately available and responsive to you. Your good is sure to come to you as you identify yourself with the spiritual qualities of success, abundance, and cooperation, allowing these qualities to express in and through you.

If you are having difficulty finding a job, dealing with a conflict at work, or feeling unfulfilled in your present position, know that you can resolve this issue through releasing limited beliefs. Spirit withholds nothing. Through an acceptance of your good, you begin to experience it.

Begin by knowing right now that you are being guided to the financially rewarding and fulfilling job or career that you desire. Feel worthy of a promotion or raise. Explore your beliefs and release any that are not constructive, replacing them with the firm conviction that, as a center in infinite Spirit, you are successful and fulfilled.

Continue to maintain an awareness of your partnership with Spirit in all that you think and do regarding your employment. Declare that there is only Spirit and that Spirit is who you are. In this way, you become an open and receptive channel for the flow of Spirit and are guided along your right path.

Ideas for Contemplation

"There is a divine plan for you. If you will open your mind to this idea and ask Spirit to reveal to you the next step for the divine plan for your life, then often the way is opened for a new unfolding to take place. Through right, constructive thinking you can direct your life."

—Catherine Ponder

"The quieter we get, the more we are able to hear from within ourselves our unique path, our own individual way of expressing Spirit. We each have a singularly unique 'karma' that leads us to use our skills, opportunities, predilections, talents, and resources in a form of service that is just right for us. The way to discover our unique path of service starts with listening inwardly and hearing what brings us joy."

—Ram Dass

"We've all had that sense of being present, being in the now, feeling ourselves to be in alignment with something larger. The feeling is one of tremendous peacefulness, gratitude, and fulfillment. And there's also a sense of excitement, because we can feel the life flowing through us. We've all had that sense of 'Ah, this is what I was born for, here I am.'"

—Joan Borysenko

"Your purpose is established in your spirit, and you come to know it through learning who you are spiritually. What is God's intention for creating you? There is a clear reason for having just one of you. You can know your purpose when you step into the mind of the Great Spirit that created you in its image and likeness. Then you can achieve anything you choose to do. Then you can have a dream bigger than you, and make it happen."

—Brother Ishmael Tetteh

Contemplate these ideas. How do you feel about them? Do these ideas open you to new ways of thinking? Are you seeing ways in which limiting beliefs have affected your experience? Record below any new awareness or insights regarding your beliefs in the life area of Employment:

Clarifying the Issue

You have become aware of limiting beliefs and are opening to new ways of thinking about your experience in the life area of Employment. Use this list of statements to clarify particular issues you want to heal through spiritual mind treatment. Circle the issues that apply to you. Write at the bottom of this page any additional issues not listed here.

I can't keep a job.

My job conflicts with my family life.

I experience discrimination at work.

I'm overlooked for promotions.

I lack career goals and direction.

I have no motivation at work.

My salary is not adequate.

I don't like the people I work with.

I'm not able to be creative in my job.

I'm nervous at job interviews.

I have conflicts with my boss.

My job is hazardous.

I'm out of work.

I have problems with child care.

I don't feel challenged at work.

I'm competing against younger people.

Other:

The Truth About You

Behind an experience of limitation is a belief in limitation. You can replace limiting beliefs by affirming the spiritual truth about you. In the list on the right are statements of spiritual truth. Use them as guides in stating the outcome you desire to realize through your spiritual mind treatment. At the bottom of the page, write the outcome you are realizing. Then use the following pages for the five steps of your spiritual mind treatment. An example of a spiritual mind treatment in the life area of Employment is on page 71.

If you have been saying:	*Now begin to say:*
I'm too stressed on my job.	I do my job calmly and easily.
I'll never get the promotion I deserve.	I receive the promotion I deserve.
I don't have any career goals.	I have clear, focused career goals.
I can't seem to keep a job.	I am a steady and committed worker.
I'm nervous on job interviews.	I do very well on job interviews.
I don't get along with my coworkers.	I am liked by my coworkers.
I don't have any job prospects.	Job offers come easily to me.
I'll never be a success.	I am successful in my job.
I'm afraid of losing my job.	I am a valued employee.
I feel inadequate as a supervisor.	I have strong skills as a supervisor.
I'm discriminated against at work.	I am treated with respect at work.
My job doesn't pay enough.	I am well paid.
My boss doesn't appreciate me.	I am appreciated by my boss.
I have trouble with child care.	I have a good support system.

Record here the outcome you are realizing through your spiritual mind treatment:

Developing Your Spiritual Mind Treatment for Employment

The following five pages are for your use in journaling about each step of your spiritual mind treatment and for exploring the language that is most meaningful to you. After you've done so, you will write your spiritual mind treatment on the page provided.

Recognition

Spirit is the essence of all that exists. Notice evidence of the presence of Spirit around you. Which spiritual qualities express the truth about your experience in the life area of Employment? Recognize the presence of these qualities in your recognition step. Write your statement of recognition here, making it as sincere and meaningful as you can. See pages 17–18 for an explanation of this step of spiritual mind treatment.

Unification

As you recognize the presence of Spirit all around you, begin now to become aware of your connection with Spirit. Feel your oneness with the qualities of Spirit. Sense these spiritual qualities in, as, and through your life. Write a statement here that expresses your awareness of your unity with Spirit. See page 19 for an explanation of this step of spiritual mind treatment.

Realization

Your statement of realization sets into motion a new cause which you experience as a new effect. By affirming the spiritual truth about you and identifying with the spiritual qualities you wish to express, you establish these qualities in and as your experience. Write your statement of realization here, including details and feelings that make it real and vivid for you. Be clear, definite, and specific. Remember to state your realization positively and to use the present tense. See pages 20-21 for an explanation of this step of spiritual mind treatment.

Thanksgiving

Giving thanks reinforces your sense of having received and accepted something. Here, with deep conviction, express your gratitude that your issue in the life area of Employment is now resolved and that your healing is already established. See pages 22-23 for an explanation of this step of spiritual mind treatment.

Release

Releasing your spiritual mind treatment directs the creative power of universal Mind, or law, to fulfill the new cause presented to it. With complete faith in the unfailing power of law, you let it go, knowing that a new cause is set in motion. You know it is done. Write your statement of release here. See pages 24–25 for an explanation of this step of spiritual mind treatment.

Your Spiritual Mind Treatment for Employment

Combined together, the statements you have written on the previous five pages comprise your complete spiritual mind treatment for the life area of Employment. Review your statements to be sure they evoke a deep feeling and conviction in you. Also make sure that the statements you have written for each of the steps of spiritual mind treatment express the intended purpose of that step. Express the essence of each step of your spiritual mind treatment here.

When you are ready, write your statements here:

Recognition:

Unification:

Realization:

Thanksgiving:

Release:

See pages 30–31 for suggestions on what to do now that you have completed your spiritual mind treatment for the life area of Employment.

Example of a Spiritual Mind Treatment for Employment

The following spiritual mind treatment is intended as a guide only. The effectiveness of your spiritual mind treatment is enhanced when you use words and statements that have the most meaning for you.

Problem to be addressed: Need for a job
Outcome: A job that meets my financial and psychological needs, providing me with an experience of abundance and fulfillment

Recognition:
I recognize God as limitless, unformed substance that is everywhere present and available. There is only the perfect life of God, and this perfect life includes and expresses as the divine qualities of abundance and joy.

Unification:
Because God is everywhere present, I am one with God. I am deeply aware of my unity with the presence and power of God. I am indivisibly linked with an infinite source. As an individualized center in the perfect life of Spirit, I express the abundance and wholeness of God.

Realization:
Right now I am accepting for myself the perfect job, one that generously meets my financial needs and is also fulfilling for me. All doubt about this in my mind now falls completely away. I feel wonderfully prosperous and abundant. I see myself going to work, getting things done, speaking with colleagues, being successful and valued as an employee, and receiving very good compensation for my work. I feel such a deep sense of fulfillment. My job is satisfying to me emotionally, and I am well compensated for my work. It is the perfect job for me, and I love doing it. My employment is perfect for me in every respect, and I am overflowing with the abundance of all good that it gives me.

Thanksgiving:
I give thanks that I am employed in the perfect work for me and that I am deriving great abundance from it. I am grateful that it is so.

Release:
I now release this word into the perfect activity of the law of Mind. I let it go, knowing that it is done in exactly the right and ideal way, and I relax with a complete sense of trust that it is done. And so it is.

MARRIAGE AND PARTNERSHIP

"Everything is part of one great harmonious whole. Once this balance is upset, once there creeps in a feeling of complete independence, then trouble starts to appear. The family unit needs to have a feeling of love permeating it, a sense of interdependence. Husband, wife, and child are bound together by a feeling of love for each other, a dependence of one on the other."

—Ernest Holmes

Marriage, or any committed partnership or relationship, joins two people in a lifelong, intimate experience of loving and caring for each other. It is an experience that involves mutual sharing and growth, working and cooperating toward common goals, and meeting the challenges of life together. Marriage, or life partnership, offers rich opportunities for joy, love, and fulfillment.

But there are many ways in which marriage or partnership can also be a source of difficulty. When challenges arise, how do you deal with them? What do you do, for example, when love seems absent and you feel alone, or when you and your partner disagree on an important issue, when you feel confined and stifled in your relationship, or when a divorce or separation has occurred? Perhaps you are not presently in a relationship and are seeking the right person to be your life partner. Spiritual mind treatment offers a way to resolve these challenges.

Whatever you may be experiencing, challenges you face in the area of marriage and life partnership are potential openings for fuller spiritual expression. When you realize that you are an individualized center in Spirit, you replace a belief in conflict and separation with the awareness of your true nature as wholeness, harmony, and love. This new awareness, deeply felt and embraced, guides you to ways in which the spiritual qualities of wholeness, harmony, and love are expressed in your life experience in the area of Marriage and Partnership.

Begin to explore the beliefs that underlie any challenge you are experiencing in the life area of Marriage and Partnership. Let go of the beliefs that are not serving you and accept the spiritual truth about you, which is wholeness and harmony. By presenting to the creative power of universal Mind the new beliefs that reflect this spiritual truth, you attract into your life an experience of wholeness and harmony.

Ideas for Contemplation

"The path of devotion is a very powerful path. It involves an initial stage of emotional relationship to some form of the beloved, then as that deepens, it moves into the stage where there is just the beloved. Everything we see is the beloved.... Finally, there is a third stage where merging occurs, and we are *the beloved."*

—Ram Dass

"When we truly embrace the sacredness of our relationships, they become real, alive experiences. Through them we pierce the veil of illusion and discover Spirit in everything."

—Deepak Chopra

"We attract what we give off, and if we're giving off a lot of heart energy and goodness, we'll attract that right back to us. We attract who we are."

—Judith Orloff

"When you change the way you look at things, the things you look at change. The more you keep your attention on peacefulness, the more you'll start looking for peace and harmony around you. And you'll find it."

—Wayne Dyer

Contemplate these ideas. How do you feel about them? Do these ideas open you to new ways of thinking? Are you seeing ways in which limiting beliefs have affected your experience? Record below any new awareness or insights regarding your beliefs in the life area of Marriage and Partnership:

Clarifying the Issue

You have become aware of limiting beliefs and are opening to new ways of thinking about your experience in the life area of Marriage and Partnership. Use this list of statements to clarify the particular issues you desire to heal through spiritual mind treatment. Circle the issues that apply to you. Write at the bottom of this page any additional issues not listed here.

I can't sustain a close relationship.

I'm afraid of commitment.

My partner doesn't do a fair share of the work.

I don't get along with my partner's family.

My partner is abusive to me.

My partner and I fight a lot.

My partner and I disagree on how to raise our children.

I don't feel loved anymore.

I can't find a life partner.

My partner and I don't spend enough time together.

My marriage is dull and routine.

My partner and I are growing apart.

My partner and I don't know how to resolve our differences.

My partner and I are not able to have children.

I'm not clear what I want in a life partner.

Other:

The Truth About You

Behind an experience of limitation is a belief in limitation. You can replace limiting beliefs by affirming the spiritual truth about you. In the list on the right are statements of spiritual truth. Use them as guides in stating the outcome you want to realize through your spiritual mind treatment. At the bottom of the page, write the outcome you are realizing. Then use the following pages for the five steps of your spiritual mind treatment. An example of a spiritual mind treatment in the life area of Marriage and Partnership is found on pages 83-84.

If you have been saying:	*Now begin to say:*
I'm bored with my relationship.	I find fulfillment in my relationship.
We never do what I want to do.	I state my needs clearly.
My partner takes me for granted.	I am valued and appreciated.
I feel stifled in my relationship.	I take time for myself.
We can't talk about our problems.	I communicate openly and well.
I have difficulty being intimate.	I easily express intimacy.
We fight a lot.	I calmly express my needs and fears.
I can't find a life partner.	I easily attract the ideal life partner.
My partner is abusive.	I value and respect myself.
We disagree about how to spend money.	My partner and I discuss our needs.
My partner works all of the time.	I express my desire for time together.
I don't like my partner's friends.	I respect our differences.
I'm not sure if marriage is right for me.	I am clear about what I want in life.

Record here the outcome you are realizing through your spiritual mind treatment:

**Developing Your Spiritual Mind Treatment
for Marriage and Partnership**

The following five pages are for your use in journaling about each step of your spiritual mind treatment and for exploring the language that is most meaningful to you. After you've done so, you will write your spiritual mind treatment on the page provided.

Recognition

Spirit is the essence of all that exists. Notice evidence of the presence of Spirit around you. Which spiritual qualities express the truth about your experience in the life area of Marriage and Partnership? Recognize the presence of these qualities in your recognition step. Write your statement of recognition here, making it as sincere and meaningful as you can. See pages 17–18 for an explanation of this step of spiritual mind treatment.

Unification

As you recognize the presence of Spirit all around you, begin now to become aware of your connection with Spirit. Feel your oneness with the qualities of Spirit. Sense these spiritual qualities in, as, and through your life. Write a statement here that expresses your awareness of your unity with Spirit. See page 19 for an explanation of this step of spiritual mind treatment.

Realization

Your statement of realization sets into motion a new cause which you experience as a new effect. By affirming the spiritual truth about you and identifying with the spiritual qualities you with to express, you establish these qualities in and as your experience. Write your statement of realization here, including details and feelings that make it real and vivid for you. Be clear, definite, and specific. Remember to state your realization positively and to use the present tense. See pages 20-21 for an explanation of this step of spiritual mind treatment.

Thanksgiving

Giving thanks reinforces your sense of having received and accepted something. Here, with deep conviction, express your gratitude that your issue in the life area of Marriage and Partnership is now resolved and that your healing is already established. See pages 22-23 for an explanation of this step of spiritual mind treatment.

Release

Releasing your spiritual mind treatment directs the creative power of universal Mind, or law, to fulfill the new cause presented to it. With complete faith in the unfailing power of law, you let it go, knowing that a new cause is set in motion. You know it is done. Write your statement of release here. See pages 24-25 for an explanation of this step of spiritual mind treatment.

Your Spiritual Mind Treatment for Marriage and Partnership

Combined together, the statements you have written on the previous five pages comprise your complete spiritual mind treatment for the life area of Marriage and Partnership. Review your statements to be sure they evoke a deep feeling and conviction in you. Also make sure that the statements you have written for each of the steps of spiritual mind treatment fulfill the intended purpose of that step. Express the essence of each step of your spiritual mind treatment here.

When you are ready, write your statements here:

Recognition:

Unification:

Realization:

Thanksgiving:

Release:

See pages 30–31 for suggestions on what to do now that you have completed your spiritual mind treatment for the life area of Marriage and Partnership.

Example of a Spiritual Mind Treatment for Marriage and Partnership

The following spiritual mind treatment is intended as a guide only. The effectiveness of your spiritual mind treatment is enhanced when you use words and statements that have the most meaning for you.

Problem to be addressed: Need to find a life partner
Outcome: Fulfilling, happy partnership with someone who shares my life goals and values

Recognition:
There is one universal life that permeates and includes all. There is one presence and one power, operating in, around, and through me and all that exists. Love is perfectly present everywhere in the universe, and is the true nature of all.

Unification:
I have a deep, inward sense of my unity with life. I am conscious right now of my true nature as Spirit. Knowing that there is only the one universal life and love everywhere present, I identify myself with it. I accept it as the reality of my being. I am an expression of perfect wholeness.

Realization:
I now realize that as an expression of Spirit I am whole and complete in every way. God withholds nothing from me and I enjoy the full measure of love and companionship in my life. The light of love shines in and through my life right now. I feel so glad, so excited, and so fulfilled by the love and companionship I now experience. How wonderful it is! I am so happy in my marriage, and it is all that I want it to be. All beliefs that have blocked this full, free acceptance of a fulfilling and happy life partnership are now released. I am attracting my perfect partner right now. That person is coming into my life at this very moment. I sense this, and feel so joyous. My life is full and rich with an ideal partner with whom to share it.

Thanksgiving:
How grateful I am for this perfect experience of love in my life! I give heartfelt thanks for the joy, fulfillment, and companionship that I experience with my ideal partner. I am so grateful.

Release:
I know that the creative power of Spirit automatically works to bring into manifestation that which I affirm in mind. There is a perfect activity that produces a like effect from a like cause. So I now release this word into the perfect activity of law and allow it to be fulfilled. With deep and total conviction, I know it is done, and so it is.

CHILDREN

"To raise children without some spiritual concept that is adequate…is going contrary to the first Law of our being, which is that we are all rooted in the Divine Spirit, in Perfect Life. We are all children of God."

—Ernest Holmes

Raising children brings many rewards. Children are loving and playful, creative and curious. Freely expressing their exuberant nature, they help us to see the world in fresh and wonderful ways. Children bring delight and joy into our lives.

When you have children, your life is enriched, but you take on a demanding responsibility. As a parent, you know that children bring joy but can also present a wide range of challenges. Most of these challenges arise from the normal day-to-day experience of raising children, and are easily met. However, some of the issues that arise are difficult ones, such as illness or serious injury, depression or hyperactivity, or failure at school. Problems such as these call forth your spiritual resources of faith, unconditional love, wisdom, and guidance.

Whatever your particular challenge with regard to raising children may be, know that all of the spiritual qualities you need to draw upon are always present within you and always available to you. Aligning your thoughts and feelings with the perfect life of Spirit, expressing in, as, and through you, you access your unlimited resources of spiritual qualities.

By consciously unifying with Spirit, the infinite source of all, you express the wisdom and patience, love and understanding of Spirit. You have access to these qualities within you because they are your essential nature. By knowing the truth of your spiritual nature, you are guided to successfully manage your child-raising issues.

Ideas for Contemplation

"Intuition is the vehicle for creativity…I strongly feel that parents should be role models for intuition, then the children can grow up believing in something natural."

—Judith Orloff

"When self-realization begins to dawn, there will no longer be so much struggle and effort. Spirit will guide us to do whatever is called for, and peace will prevail. This first happens within individuals, and then it happens to relationships based on Spirit, until finally it extends to whole families and societies."

—Deepak Chopra

"When children say a positive word about themselves and act it out, then they embody it. In this way children learn to feel empowered and they also learn to recognize their individual gifts and talents."

—Brother Ishmael Tetteh

Contemplate these ideas. How do you feel about them? Do these ideas open you to new ways of thinking? Are you seeing ways in which limiting beliefs have affected your experience? Record below any new awareness or insights regarding your beliefs in the life area of Children:

Clarifying the Issue

You have become aware of limiting beliefs and are opening to new ways of thinking about your experience in the life area of Children. Use this list of statements to clarify the particular issues you want to heal through spiritual mind treatment. Circle the issues that apply to you. Write at the bottom of this page any additional issues not listed here.

I don't have enough time with my children.

My children and I argue a lot.

I can't cope with my child's illness.

Raising my child alone is hard.

I don't have any time for myself.

I'm afraid my child is using drugs.

I don't know how to set limits for my child.

I can't get my children to study.

My partner doesn't help with the children.

I worry a lot about my children.

My child is having problems at school.

I'm afraid to discipline my children.

I feel like I neglect my children.

My teenager is moody and rude.

Our children are causing a strain in our marriage.

I am having a hard time getting pregnant.

Other:

The Truth About You

Behind an experience of limitation is a belief in limitation. You can replace limiting beliefs by affirming the spiritual truth about you. In the list on the right are statements of spiritual truth. Use them as guides in stating the outcome you desire to realize through your spiritual mind treatment. At the bottom of the page, write the outcome you are realizing. Then use the following pages for the five steps of your spiritual mind treatment. An example of a spiritual mind treatment in the life area of Children is found on pages 95-96

If you have been saying:	*Now begin to say:*
I'm not a good parent.	I am a strong, capable parent.
I'm afraid my child is using drugs.	My child is safe from harm.
My child is having problems at school.	I help my child deal with problems.
I don't discipline my children well.	I guide my children wisely.
I don't have enough time with my child.	I spend quality time with my child.
I'm having problems raising my child alone.	I have the help and support I need.
My partner and I fight about child-raising.	My partner and I resolve our issues.
I don't know how to set limits.	I am able to take care of my children.
I can't provide well for my children.	I meet our financial needs.
The baby is putting stress on our marriage.	My partner and I have time together.
I feel guilty about neglecting my children.	I pay loving attention to my children.
My teenager and I always disagree.	I understand my teenager.
I don't want my children to leave home.	My life is filled with love and joy.

Record here the outcome you are realizing through your spiritual mind treatment:

Developing Your Spiritual Mind Treatment for Children

The following five pages are for your use in journaling about each step of your spiritual mind treatment and for exploring the language that is most meaningful to you. After you've done so, you will write your spiritual mind treatment on the page provided.

Recognition

Spirit is the essence of all that exists. Notice evidence of the presence of Spirit around you. Which spiritual qualities express the truth about your experience in the life area of Children? Recognize the presence of these qualities in your recognition step. Write your statement of recognition here, making it as sincere and meaningful as you can. See pages 17–18 for an explanation of this step of spiritual mind treatment.

Unification

As you recognize the presence of Spirit all around you, begin now to become aware of your connection with Spirit. Feel your oneness with the qualities of Spirit. Sense these spiritual qualities in, as, and through your life. Write a statement here that expresses your awareness of your unity with Spirit. See page 19 for an explanation of this step of spiritual mind treatment.

Realization

Your statement of realization sets into motion a new cause which you experience as a new effect. By affirming the spiritual truth about you and identifying with the spiritual qualities you wish to express, you establish these qualities in and as your experience. Write your statement of realization here, including details and feelings that make it real and vivid for you. Be clear, definite, and specific. Remember to state your realization positively and in the present tense. See pages 20-21 for an explanation of this step of spiritual mind treatment.

Thanksgiving

Giving thanks reinforces your sense of having received and accepted something. Here, with deep conviction, express your gratitude that your issue in the life area of Children is now resolved and that your healing is already established. See pages 22-23 for an explanation of this step of spiritual mind treatment.

Release

Releasing your spiritual mind treatment directs the creative power of universal Mind, or law, to fulfill the new cause presented to it. With complete faith in the unfailing power of law, you let it go, knowing that a new cause is set in motion. You know it is done. Write your statement of release here. See pages 24-25 for an explanation of this step of spiritual mind treatment.

Your Spiritual Mind Treatment for Children

Combined together, the statements you have written on the previous five pages comprise your complete spiritual mind treatment for the life area of Children. Review your statements to be sure they evoke a deep feeling and conviction in you. Also make sure that the statements you have written for each of the steps of spiritual mind treatment fulfill the intended purpose of that step. Express the essence of each step of your spiritual mind treatment here.

When you are ready, write your statements here:

Recognition:

Unification:

Realization:

Thanksgiving:

Release:

See pages 30–31 for suggestions on what to do now that you have completed your spiritual mind treatment for the life area of Children.

Example of a Spiritual Mind Treatment for Children

The following spiritual mind treatment is intended as a guide only. The effectiveness of your spiritual mind treatment is enhanced when you use words and statements that have the most meaning for you.

Problem to be addressed: Fear about my child's safety
Outcome: Peace of mind about my child's safety and well-being

Recognition:
I know there is only one life and one Spirit, in, as, and through all. I recognize right now the whole and one reality, present in, as, and through all. I recognize life as one harmonious unity which includes all that is or ever was. Spirit, the true nature of all, guides, guards, and protects all. Spirit is the perfect love that is everywhere present.

Unification:
Because Spirit is all, It can have nothing outside of Itself. It is one perfect and harmonious whole, and I am part of this whole. I can never be separate from It. Knowing that Spirit is my true nature, I now consciously identify myself as an expression of Spirit and release all belief or feeling that I am in any way separate from It. I am an undivided center in the universal Mind. All of the qualities of Spirit are true of me, including peace and protection. This is also the true nature of my child.

Realization:
There is only Spirit and the truth of Spirit is peace and protection. All of life is protected, guided, and guarded. Instead of seeing danger or being fearful, I now see that Spirit is present everywhere. My new attitude is one of faith and peace. I relax into the deep knowing that Spirit is present in, as, and through my child. Where I had seen potential harm, I now see only peace and harmony. All fear is now released. I realize a new understanding in my mind and I am free of all fear for the safety and well-being of my child. I sense deeply the presence of peace and harmony as the life of my child. I feel completely at peace.

Thanksgiving:
I give thanks for my child's safety and well-being. With deep gratitude, I completely accept the healing of my concern for my child, knowing that all is well.

Release:

Allowing this treatment to go forth into the creative medium of Spirit, I release it joyously for the law to do its perfect work. I know that my word returns to me fulfilled. It is done. And so it is.

PARENTS

"I believe we are all one family in Spirit, and that Spirit is working in each of us in such a way that there will be produced a better family, a better world.... Spirit is the Father and Mother of all. Our earthly parents symbolize this heavenly parentage."

—Ernest Holmes

As an adult, you begin to see your parents more objectively than you did when you were a child. While they once may have seemed either infallible or deficient, now you are able to view them more realistically, as people with their own hopes and fears, strengths and weaknesses, who did the best they could. You have begun to appreciate them for what they gave you.

However, even with a greater appreciation for them than you had during your younger years, you may find that your life is still affected by your childhood relationship with your parents. Negative experiences from the past can limit the free and full expression of your true nature as Spirit if those experiences implanted in you limiting beliefs about your capabilities or worth.

Beliefs you developed about yourself when you were young may be causing you to remain overly dependent on others, to be intimidated by people in authority, or to feel guilt over past behavior disapproved of by your parents. These are issues that can be healed when you use spiritual mind treatment to release limiting beliefs and realize the truth of who you are.

The problem you face may relate to something that has arisen recently. Perhaps you are caring for an aging or ill parent and are finding this responsibility to be overwhelming. Through spiritual mind treatment you can access the spiritual qualities of support and energy which are fully present within you and always available to you.

Spirit is your true essence, so whatever is true of Spirit is also true of you. Knowing you are an expression of Spirit leads you to release limiting beliefs and to express who you truly are. Spiritual mind treatment can help you to realize peace and harmony with regard to your relationship with your parents.

Ideas for Contemplation

"If you can't forgive, just release, turn loose, and keep doing that until whatever it is fades away. The bad feeling leaves, and often you can begin to see the situation from the other person's point of view, which helps you to understand why the situation happened."
—Catherine Ponder

"Everybody's doing the best they can, and your parents were raised by the people they were raised by, and that's the source for their information on how to handle stuff."
—Louise Hay

"We can't come to forgiveness as long as we're holding on to a grievance story. Each of us is a free person who is larger than any story of our past."
—Joan Borysenko

"When we truly embrace the sacredness of our relationships, they become real, alive experiences. Through them we pierce the veil of illusion and discover Spirit in everything. We experience more laughter, more peace and harmony, and greater affection for the people around us."
—Deepak Chopra

Contemplate these ideas. How do you feel about them? Do these ideas open you to new ways of thinking? Are you seeing ways in which limiting beliefs have affected your experience? Record below any new awareness or insights regarding your beliefs in the life area of Parents:

Clarifying the Issue

You have become aware of limiting beliefs and are opening to new ways of thinking about your experience in the life area of Parents. Use this list of statements to clarify the particular issues you want to heal through spiritual mind treatment. Circle the issues that apply to you. Write at the bottom of this page any additional issues not listed here.

My parents are a financial burden.

I'm concerned about my parent's illness.

My parents try to control me.

I don't like the person my parent is married to now.

Nothing I do satisfies my parents.

My parents are too dependent on me.

I can't forgive my parents for some things.

It bothers me to put my parent in a nursing home.

My parents and I fight a lot.

I can't talk honestly with my parents.

My parents interfere with my relationship with my partner.

I'm angry about my parents' divorce.

I don't want my parent to live with me.

My parents expect too much of me.

My parents try to live their lives through me.

Other:

The Truth About You

Behind an experience of limitation is a belief in limitation. You can replace limiting beliefs by affirming the spiritual truth about you. In the list on the right are statements of spiritual truth. Use them as guides in stating the outcome you desire to realize through your spiritual mind treatment. At the bottom of the page, write the outcome you are realizing. Then use the following pages for the five steps of your spiritual mind treatment. An example of a spiritual mind treatment in the life area of Parents is found on page 107.

If you have been saying:	*Now begin to say:*
My parents treat me like a child.	I freely make my own decisions.
My mother still tries to control me.	I am independent of my mother.
My parents are a financial burden.	I have all of the resources I need.
I'm angry over my parents' divorce.	I accept that I am safe and loved.
My parents never understand me.	I communicate well with my parents.
I'm worn out by my parent's illness.	I receive help with my parent's care.
I can't forgive my parent's alcoholism.	I feel compassion for my parent.
My parents and I always argue.	We discuss our differences calmly.
I regret not having loved my parents more.	I love and honor my parents today.
My parents are too dependent on me.	I am free to live my own life.
My parents are too critical of me.	I accept and love myself.
I'm never good enough for my parents.	I am exactly the way I need to be.
My parents live their lives through me.	I am free to live my own life.
My parents and I are estranged.	I feel at peace with my parents.
I am afraid of putting my parent in a home.	I accept the best care for my parent.

Record here the outcome you are realizing through your spiritual mind treatment:

Developing Your Spiritual Mind Treatment for Parents

The following five pages are for your use in journaling about each step of your spiritual mind treatment and for exploring the language that is most meaningful to you. After you've done so, you will write your spiritual mind treatment on the page provided.

Recognition

Spirit is the essence of all that exists. Notice evidence of the presence of Spirit around you. Which spiritual qualities express the truth about your experience in the life area of Parents? Recognize the presence of these qualities in your recognition step. Write your statement of recognition here, making it as sincere and meaningful as you can. See pages 17–18 for an explanation of this step of spiritual mind treatment.

Unification

As you recognize the presence of Spirit all around you, begin now to become aware of your connection with Spirit. Feel your oneness with the qualities of Spirit. Sense these spiritual qualities in, as, and through your life. Write a statement here that expresses your awareness of your unity with Spirit. See page 19 for an explanation of this step of spiritual mind treatment.

Realization

Your statement of realization sets into motion a new cause which you experience as a new effect. By affirming the spiritual truth about you, and identifying with the spiritual qualities you wish to express, you establish these qualities in and as your experience. Write your statement of realization here, including details and feelings that make it real and vivid for you. Be clear, definite, and specific. Remember to state your realization positively and to use the present tense. See pages 20-21 for an explanation of this step of spiritual mind treatment.

Thanksgiving

Giving thanks reinforces your sense of having received and accepted something. Here, with deep conviction, express your gratitude that your issue in the life area of Parents is now resolved and that your healing is already established. See pages 22-23 for an explanation of this step of spiritual mind treatment.

Release

Releasing your spiritual mind treatment directs the creative power of universal Mind, or law, to fulfill the new cause presented to it. With complete faith in the unfailing power of law, you let it go, knowing that a new cause is set in motion. You know it is done. Write your statement of release here. See pages 24–25 for an explanation of this step of spiritual mind treatment.

Your Spiritual Mind Treatment for Parents

Combined together, the statements you have written on the previous five pages comprise your complete spiritual mind treatment for the life area of Parents. Review your statements to be sure they evoke a deep feeling and conviction in you. Also make sure that the statements you have written for each of the steps of spiritual mind treatment fulfill the intended purpose of that step. Express the essence of each step of your spiritual mind treatment here.

When you are ready, write your statements here:

Recognition:

Unification:

Realization:

Thanksgiving:

Release:

See pages 30-31 for suggestions on what to do now that you have completed your spiritual mind treatment for the life area of Parents.

Example of a Spiritual Mind Treatment for Parents

The following spiritual mind treatment is intended as a guide only. The effectiveness of your spiritual mind treatment is enhanced when you use words and statements that have the most meaning for you.

Problem to be addressed: Anger at parents
Outcome: Forgiveness of parents and release of the past

Recognition:
I recognize that good is all there is. There is nothing except good. It is the one truth, the one life, and it is always whole and perfect. Good is everywhere present, expressing as harmony, freedom, and love. There is only good.

Unification:
I know that the omnipresent good is the truth of my being. It is in me, as me, and I live, move, and have my being in this infinite good. The one perfect life that permeates all is my life right now and always. I am an individualized expression of the harmony, freedom and love that are the truth of the eternal good.

Realization:
I now speak my word for the complete release of the past and for forgiveness of all events and experiences in the past that hurt me in any way. A new experience of life is opening for me. In place of anger I realize peace and love. I am free right now of all anger. I am completely free from all burden of the past. I have no reservation or doubt about my worth and value. I know I am loved, and I freely and easily release everything unlike the love and harmony that are the absolute truth of my life and being. I forgive all events, experiences, persons, places, and things that have seemed to limit my expression of love, peace, joy, and abundance. Right now I experience my life as completely free and joyous. I feel renewed. My life flows with love. All is well.

Thanksgiving:
I feel so grateful for this wonderful truth and give joyful thanks for the great good I now experience as forgiveness. With heartfelt gratitude, I say thank you.

Release:
I now release this word into the perfect activity of the law of Mind, knowing that a new cause is set into motion. I trust in the law completely and release this treatment, knowing it is done. And so it is!

FRIENDSHIP

"Friendship and all harmonious relationship with others can only be established through love, affection, and kindness.... To the extent that we know that love and harmony are the nature of God, and permit them to flow through us, to that extent will our relations with others be harmonious."

—Ernest Holmes

There is a bond that draws you to certain people. You can sense this connection, even when meeting someone for the first time. There is a feeling of rapport, a deep awareness of being seen and understood. This is the nature of friendship.

Friendship offers an opportunity to know yourself more completely and at a deeper level. It also calls you to be caring and supportive toward another. For these reasons friendship is one of life's most valued experiences.

Friendship calls forth the spiritual qualities of love, kindness, support, and understanding. These qualities come freely when your interactions with friends are smooth and harmonious. However, there may also be times of misunderstanding or disharmony. If this is an issue in your life, you can use spiritual mind treatment to recognize the presence of Spirit in, as, and through both you and your friend. In this way you turn your attention away from disharmony and embrace your oneness with the perfect harmony of Spirit.

If you wish to attract more friends into your life, know that you express the qualities of love, understanding, acceptance, and support. By allowing these qualities to express through you, you attract a like experience of them into your life.

Use spiritual mind treatment to establish within yourself a firm conviction of your true nature as these qualities. Realize and embody the presence of Spirit, and sense your unity with all people. As you do so, any problem you may have in the area of Friendship is resolved, and your life is enriched with close, loving friendships.

Ideas for Contemplation

"When our thoughts are not peaceful, we tend to attract experiences that are not peaceful. We get what we consistently think about, whether we want it or not. The more you keep your attention on peacefulness, the more you'll start looking for harmony and peace around you. And you'll find it."

—Wayne Dyer

"We all know that there are all kinds of friendships, and some friendships are healthy and some are not. Some support you in being a victim, in staying stuck in your most egoic and constricted self. Other friendships support your growth in gratitude and mindfulness, prayerfulness and awakening. Life is difficult and we need people who help to keep us on course."

—Joan Borysenko

"A collective human 'pain-body' contains the pain suffered by countless human beings throughout history. Periodically the pain-body becomes activated and seeks more suffering to feed on. If you are not absolutely present, it takes over your mind and feeds on negative thinking as well as negative experiences such as drama in human relationships."

—Eckhart Tolle

Contemplate these ideas. How do you feel about them? Do these ideas open you to new ways of thinking? Are you seeing ways in which limiting beliefs have affected your experience? Record below any new awareness or insights regarding your beliefs in the life area of Friendship:

Clarifying the Issue

You have become aware of limiting beliefs and are opening to new ways of thinking about your experience in the life area of Friendship. Use this list of statements to clarify the particular issues you want to heal through spiritual mind treatment. Circle the issues that apply to you. Write at the bottom of this page any additional issues not listed here.

I can't seem to keep friends.

I don't have any close friends.

I can't tell my friends my true feelings.

I'm afraid to get close to people.

My friend asks too much of me.

I feel like my friend is just using me.

I'm afraid to disagree with my friend.

I don't have time for friendships.

I don't know how to make friends.

I feel lonely.

My friends are doing things I don't like.

I'm jealous of my friends.

I haven't been a good friend.

I feel shut out by my friends.

I let my friends down.

I'm hurt by my friend's betrayal.

Other:

The Truth About You

Behind an experience of limitation is a belief in limitation. You can replace limiting beliefs by affirming the spiritual truth about you. In the list on the right are statements of spiritual truth. Use them as guides in stating the outcome you desire to realize through your spiritual mind treatment. At the bottom of the page, write the outcome you are realizing. Then use the following pages for the five steps of your spiritual mind treatment. An example of a spiritual mind treatment in the life area of Friendship is found on pages 119-120.

If you have been saying:	*Now begin to say:*
I have trouble keeping friends.	I am a loyal friend.
I don't know how to make new friends.	I reach out to people in trust.
I let friends take advantage of me.	I respect my boundaries.
I'm afraid of close friendships.	I am open to loving friendships.
I feel left out by my friends.	I am a loved and valued friend.
I'm jealous of my friends.	All of my needs are easily met.
I am upset with my friend.	I am understood and cared about.
I'm afraid my friend will betray me.	I am a true and trustworthy friend.
My friends often let me down.	I release expectations of others.
My friend makes too many demands.	I freely choose what I want to do.
My friend is not honest with me.	I share my feelings openly.
I don't feel worthy of close friendships.	I am a loved and loving person.
I don't enjoy the friends I have.	I enjoy my life and like who I am.
I can't break off a harmful friendship.	I am free to do what is best for me.
My friend didn't come through for me.	I have all the support I need.

Record here the outcome you are realizing through your spiritual mind treatment:

Developing Your Spiritual Mind Treatment for Friendship

The following five pages are for your use in journaling about each step of your spiritual mind treatment and for exploring the language that is most meaningful to you. After you've done so, you will write your spiritual mind treatment on the page provided.

Recognition

Spirit is the essence of all that exists. Notice evidence of the presence of Spirit around you. Which spiritual qualities express the truth about your experience in the life area of Friendship? Recognize the presence of these qualities in your recognition step. Write your statement of recognition here, making it as sincere and meaningful as you can. See pages 17–18 for an explanation of this step of spiritual mind treatment.

Unification

As you recognize the presence of Spirit all around you, begin now to become aware of your connection with Spirit. Feel your oneness with the qualities of Spirit. Sense these spiritual qualities in, as, and through your life. Write a statement here that expresses your awareness of your unity with Spirit. See page 19 for an explanation of this step of spiritual mind treatment.

Realization

Your statement of realization sets into motion a new cause which you experience as a new effect. By affirming the spiritual truth about you, and identifying with the spiritual qualities you wish to express, you establish these qualities in and as your experience. Write your statement of realization here, including details and feelings that make it real and vivid for you. Be clear, definite, and specific. Remember to state your realization positively and to use the present tense. See pages 20-21 for an explanation of this step of spiritual mind treatment.

Thanksgiving

Giving thanks reinforces your sense of having received and accepted something. Here, with deep conviction, express your gratitude that your issue in the life area of Friendship is now resolved and that your healing is already established. See pages 22-23 for an explanation of this step of spiritual mind treatment.

Release

Releasing your spiritual mind treatment directs the creative power of universal Mind, or law, to fulfill the new cause presented to it. With complete faith in the unfailing power of law, you let it go, knowing that a new cause is set in motion. You know it is done. Write your statement of release here. See pages 24-25 for an explanation of this step of spiritual mind treatment.

Your Spiritual Mind Treatment for Friendship

Combined together, the statements you have written on the previous five pages comprise your complete spiritual mind treatment for the life area of Friendship. Review your statements to be sure they evoke a deep feeling and conviction in you. Also make sure that the statements you have written for each of the steps of spiritual mind treatment fulfill the intended purpose of that step. Express the essence of each step of your spiritual mind treatment here.

When you are ready, write your statements here:

Recognition:

Unification:

Realization:

Thanksgiving:

Release:

See pages 30-31 for suggestions on what to do now that you have completed your spiritual mind treatment for the life area of Friendship.

Example of a Spiritual Mind Treatment for Friendship

The following spiritual mind treatment is intended as a guide only. The effectiveness of your spiritual mind treatment is enhanced when you use words and statements that have the most meaning for you.

Purpose of Treatment: Need for friendship
Outcome of Treatment: Active involvement with and enjoyment of friends

Recognition:
There is one infinite presence everywhere. It is Spirit. It is all. There is only this unity. All is connected and comes from the one source, which is perfect wholeness. I know that oneness is the truth about life and about me. I now recognize this perfect wholeness as being everywhere present and in, as, and through everything.

Unification:
Knowing that Spirit is the ultimate truth of all that exists and is universally present, I know that I am an individualized center in Spirit. I partake of the nature and essence of this wholeness. I am one with the spiritual qualities of love, caring, companionship, and joy.

Realization:
Today I go forth in joy, knowing that everyone is my friend, knowing that I am a friend to all people. I let go of all thought of lack in my life. I open myself to friendship, with a sincere desire to give and receive love. My life is a communion of Spirit with Spirit. I know that the one Spirit, the one life that is in, as, and through all people, is my life now, and my life is filled with friends I love and who love me. I believe in and accept a greater good than I have ever experienced. I have an inward sense of peace and joy. There is no anxiety or sense of being alone, for I know I am surrounded by love. I live now with an inner assurance of being one with all of life and with all people. Caring friends are attracted to me, because I am filled with the love that forever emanates from the living Spirit within me. I now express and accept loving friendship as my experience.

Thanksgiving:
How wonderful it is to have the gift of friendship! I am so grateful for this experience of friendship in my life. My heart is full of thanks for loving friends and caring companionship. I accept this new experience with deep gratitude.

Release:

Accepting with complete faith that a new cause has been set in motion, I now release this word to the perfect activity of creative Mind, letting go and allowing this power to bring into manifestation that which I declare. I know my word returns to me fulfilled. It is done, and so it is.

EMOTIONAL WELL-BEING

"If you will take time daily to sense the Presence of Life within you, believe in it, and accept it, before long the life you have known until now will gradually disappear. Something new and wonderful will be born—a bigger, better, and more perfect life. You will pass from sadness into happiness, from lack and want into greater freedom, and from fear into faith; and from a sense of being alone and isolated in the universe you will realize that you are one with all Life."

—Ernest Holmes

Emotional well-being is a state of being mentally and spiritually at peace. It means having the emotional strength and inner resources to deal with whatever comes along in your life. To experience emotional well-being is to have a healthy attitude of self-acceptance. You feel good about who you are, are inwardly at peace, and meet the everyday challenges of living with ease and confidence.

From time to time, difficult feelings such as confusion or anxiety arise for everyone, but these down periods are brief when you know the truth of your spiritual nature. You return easily to your center and feel connected with your source. A life grounded in emotional well-being is one that works well. It is a life in which the spiritual qualities within you are expressing freely.

Spirit, the source of all peace, is always within you and is never apart from you. Opening to the presence of Spirit in your life is the foundation of emotional well-being. In spiritual mind treatment you realize that you are a whole, complete, and perfect expression of Spirit. You release limited beliefs and replace them with new beliefs about yourself that are the truth about you. Universal Mind responds to your realization of peace by attracting peaceful experiences into your life.

To experience the peace and serenity that are the foundation of emotional well-being, you need only realize your oneness with these spiritual qualities. The life of Spirit is always within you. You can always access it.

Ideas for Contemplation

"If we think of ourselves as expressions of God, then that means that we are not inadequate. It means in God's mind we are strong and not weak, clear and not confused, healthy and not sick. As different levels of our consciousness receive that information and we embrace it as a truth we embody, not merely an intellectual concept, we are permeated by a new self-perception."

—Marianne Williamson

"All spiritual growth, 100 percent of it, is about releasing or eliminating rather than attaining something, because we're already It spiritually. So it's always a good sign when we start to hit bottom. Something's being dissolved, transformed, redeemed."

—Michael Bernard Beckwith

"For years I lived in depression and anxiety. One night I couldn't stand it any longer. The thought came into my mind, 'I cannot live with myself any longer.' I stood back from the thought and asked, 'Who is the self that I cannot live with?' In that moment, that mind-based sense of self collapsed. What remained was I—not the form 'I,' not the story-based 'I'—but a deeper sense of being, of presence."

—Eckhart Tolle

"Even though I had quite a nice childhood, I still suffered from unworthiness, which is a collective, societal wound, rather than just a personal one. In healing this wound and finding a sense of self-worth, I opened my heart. We work on opening our hearts through forgiveness, surrendering to God, and seeing God everywhere—in ourselves and other people."

—Joan Borysenko

Contemplate these ideas. How do you feel about them? Do these ideas open you to new ways of thinking? Are you seeing ways in which limiting beliefs have affected your experience? Record below any new awareness or insights regarding your beliefs in the life area of Emotional Well-Being:

Clarifying the Issue

You have become aware of limiting beliefs and are opening to new ways of thinking about your experience in the life area of Emotional Well-Being. Use this list of statements to clarify the particular issues you want to heal through spiritual mind treatment. Circle the issues that apply to you. Write at the bottom of this page any additional issues not listed here.

I experience a lot of anxiety.

I can't express my feelings.

I'm unhappy with my life.

No one understands me.

I can't stop worrying.

I get upset and frustrated easily.

I feel like a failure.

I have a lot of shame.

I'm fearful much of the time.

I just don't know who I am.

I can't get over past hurts.

I feel shy around people.

I have a lot of anger.

No one ever listens to me.

My life doesn't matter.

I don't feel loved.

Other:

The Truth About You

Behind an experience of limitation is a belief in limitation. You can replace limiting beliefs by affirming the spiritual truth about you. In the list on the right are statements of spiritual truth. Use them as guides in stating the outcome you desire to realize through your spiritual mind treatment. At the bottom of the page, write the outcome you are realizing. Then use the following pages for the five steps of your spiritual mind treatment. An example of a spiritual mind treatment in the life area of Emotional Well-Being is found on page 131.

If you have been saying:	*Now begin to say:*
I am easily frustrated.	I let every situation flow smoothly.
I can't help feeling anxious.	I know that I am safe.
I'm afraid to try new things.	I have the courage to try new things.
I feel intimidated by others.	I am poised and centered.
I get angry a lot.	I feel supported by life.
I feel guilty about my past actions.	I accept myself with love.
I am often confused.	I feel inwardly peaceful and clear.
I'm filled with resentment.	I am safe and my needs are met.
I feel tense and nervous all the time.	I relax and trust life.
I'm a failure.	I am a success at being myself.
I feel empty inside.	I am connected with all of life.
No one understands me.	I am valued and appreciated.
I can't express my feelings.	I am worthy of being heard.
I want to hide from life.	I am strong and capable.
I worry all the time.	Everything in my life is secure.

Record here the outcome you are realizing through your spiritual mind treatment:

Developing Your Spiritual Mind Treatment for Emotional Well–Being

The following five pages are for your use in journaling about each step of your spiritual mind treatment and for exploring the language that is most meaningful to you. After you've done so, you will write your spiritual mind treatment on the page provided.

Recognition

Spirit is the essence of all that exists. Notice evidence of the presence of Spirit around you. Which spiritual qualities express the truth about your experience in the life area of Emotional Well–Being? Recognize the presence of these qualities in your recognition step. Write your statement of recognition here, making it as sincere and meaningful as you can. See pages 17–18 for an explanation of this step of spiritual mind treatment.

Unification

As you recognize the presence of Spirit all around you, begin now to become aware of your connection with Spirit. Feel your oneness with the qualities of Spirit. Sense these spiritual qualities in, as, and through your life. Write a statement here that expresses your awareness of your unity with Spirit. See page 19 for an explanation of this step of spiritual mind treatment.

Realization

Your statement of realization sets into motion a new cause which you experience as a new effect. By affirming the spiritual truth about you, and identifying with the spiritual qualities you wish to express, you establish these qualities in and as your experience. Write your statement of realization here, including details and feelings that make it real and vivid for you. Be clear, definite, and specific. Remember to state your realization positively and to use the present tense. See pages 20-21 for an explanation of this step of spiritual mind treatment.

Thanksgiving

Giving thanks reinforces your sense of having received and accepted something. Here, with deep conviction, express your gratitude that your issue in the life area of Emotional Well-Being is now resolved and that your healing is already established. See pages 22-23 for an explanation of this step of spiritual mind treatment.

Release

Releasing your spiritual mind treatment directs the creative power of universal Mind, or law, to fulfill the new cause presented to it. With complete faith in the unfailing power of law, you let it go, knowing that a new cause is set in motion. You know it is done. Write your statement of release here. See pages 24–25 for an explanation of this step of spiritual mind treatment.

Your Spiritual Mind Treatment for Emotional Well-Being

Combined together, the statements you have written on the previous five pages comprise your complete spiritual mind treatment for the life area of Emotional Well-Being. Review your statements to be sure they evoke a deep feeling and conviction in you. Also make sure that the statements you have written for each of the steps of spiritual mind treatment fulfill the intended purpose of that step. Express the essence of each step of your spiritual mind treatment here.

When you are ready, write your statements here:

Recognition:

Unification:

Realization:

Thanksgiving:

Release:

See pages 30–31 for suggestions on what to do now that you have completed your spiritual mind treatment for the life area of Emotional Well-Being.

Example of a Spiritual Mind Treatment for Emotional Well-Being

The following spiritual mind treatment is intended as a guide only. The effectiveness of your spiritual mind treatment is enhanced when you use words and statements that have the most meaning for you.

Problem to be addressed: Feelings of anxiety
Outcome: An ongoing sense of peace and poise

Recognition:
All of life is one. It is perfect peace and harmony. Life expresses and operates through all that exists as peace and harmony. There is an abiding calm and stillness at the center of everything. The source of all is the one Mind, one Spirit.

Unification:
I am one with Spirit. Spirit expresses in and through me because I am part of Spirit. I am inseparably connected with an infinite intelligence. There is only oneness, and I am conscious right now of being a center in the peace and poise of Spirit.

Realization:
I accept my divine nature. I enter into a full awareness of my partnership with the peace, harmony, poise, and love that are the essence of Spirit. They are my essence, too. I am no longer afraid of anything in life. A deep and abiding sense of calm permeates my being. All is well. I feel this and know it. The peace and power of Spirit manifest in my life as right decisions, calm emotions, joyful relationships, and an overall sense that everything is in perfect order. I relax into this deep knowing, allowing it to spread throughout my mind and body. All of my activities flow easily and well. Nothing disturbs or upsets me. I see and experience the love, guidance and peace of Spirit at all times.

Thanksgiving:
I give thanks as I gratefully accept this truth about my life, knowing I am always centered in the heart of goodness.

Release:
Accepting the fullness of good as my life experience, I release this word of faith to the perfect activity of the universal law. That which I now realize is perfectly established. It is done. And so it is.

ADDICTION

"The truth about my real Self reveals to my mind a complete freedom from any habit that could rob me of peace or of my rightful mentality."

—Ernest Holmes

Addictive behavior is often a way to escape from feelings. The person who practices an addiction is retreating from life, becoming dependent on a substance, an activity or even another person, as a way to ease pain or manage fear.

If pursued as a way of escape, any kind of compulsive behavior can prevent you from experiencing fulfillment, joy and peace of mind. This is so because compulsive behavior blocks the expression of your real self. When you are attuned to your real self, which is Spirit, you naturally express the qualities of joy and peace.

Addictions often result from feelings of shame, guilt or unworthiness. When you recognize the presence of Spirit in and as your life, you replace these feelings with a new understanding of the spiritual truth about you. This process of releasing old, limited self-concepts leads to the revealing of who you truly are as Spirit in expression. As you align your thinking in this new way, you call forth the peace, power and freedom that have always been inherent within you. You then attract into your life new circumstances that reflect these qualities of Spirit in and as you.

Explore the fears and limited beliefs that lie behind the addictive behaviors that have restricted your experience of life, and be willing to release those fears and beliefs. Affirm the truth about yourself. You are Spirit in expression and you possess all of the qualities of Spirit. You can experience peace, freedom and fulfillment, because that is who and what you are.

Ideas for Contemplation

"Bondage is conditioned behavior. Freedom is found by practicing life-centered, present moment awareness, which means to be in the moment and to explore the moment, the creativity of the moment, and also to observe our addictive behavior without judgment."

—Deepak Chopra

"Listening to our intuition allows us to do things that are very good for us energetically. So instead of being driven by your mind and a compulsion, take a minute to listen to your intuition and ask, 'What's good for me?' Learn how to generate positive emotional energy and deflect negativity."

—Judith Orloff

"The most important thing you can do in life is to transform your main character—to create a wonderful story about what you believe about yourself. It is the way of creating heaven for yourself, instead of that hell that many people have when they don't like the main character of their story. When you look in the mirror and hate what you see, you need addictions to survive."

—Don Miguel Ruiz

"Every time you look in the mirror, don't ask, 'What's wrong?' Say, 'I love you.' It makes a big difference in your life."

—Louise Hay

Contemplate these ideas. How do you feel about them? Do these ideas open you to new ways of thinking? Are you seeing ways in which limiting beliefs have affected your experience? Record below any new awareness or insights regarding your beliefs in the life area of Addiction:

Clarifying the Issue

You have become aware of limiting beliefs and are opening to new ways of thinking about your experience in the life area of Addiction. Use this list of statements to clarify the particular issues you want to heal through spiritual mind treatment. Circle the issues that apply to you. Write at the bottom of this page any additional issues not listed here.

I can't give up taking tranquilizers.

My drinking is out of control.

I spend too much time on the Internet.

I watch television as a way to escape from life.

All I eat is junk food.

I can't stop smoking.

I spend all of my time working.

I can't relax until my house is spotless.

My credit cards are charged up to the maximum.

I can't control my gambling.

I have a compulsion to exercise for hours every day.

I feel uneasy unless everything is in order.

I drink a lot of coffee all day long.

I play video games until late at night.

I'm afraid I'll resume using drugs.

I feel trapped in an abusive relationship.

I'm always buying things I don't need.

Other:

The Truth About You

Behind an experience of limitation is a belief in limitation. You can replace limiting beliefs by affirming the spiritual truth about you. In the list on the right are statements of spiritual truth. Use them as guides in stating the outcome you want to realize through your spiritual mind treatment. At the bottom of the page, write the outcome you are realizing. Then use the following pages for the five steps of your spiritual mind treatment. An example of a spiritual mind treatment in the life area of Addiction is on pages 143-144.

If you have been saying:	*Now begin to say:*
I can't live without my tranquilizers.	I am calm and at ease with myself.
I'm hooked on Internet surfing.	I enjoy a variety of activities.
I can't control my eating.	I make good dietary decisions.
I need to drink to feel at ease.	I handle situations calmly.
Life is exciting only when I gamble.	I am at peace with myself.
I can't stop smoking.	I am able to relax without smoking.
I watch television as an escape.	My life is rich and full.
I can't take any time off from work.	I enjoy a varied, balanced life.
I eat too much junk food.	I am loved and valued.
I need to have everything perfect.	I am at peace with the flow of life.
I'm in an abusive relationship.	I am worthy of love and respect.
My credit card use is out of control.	I am enough and my life is full.
I can't get to sleep without pills.	I am completely safe and secure.
I need to drink to feel at ease.	I love and accept who I am.
I haven't taken a vacation in years.	I am free to relax and have fun.
I can't quit smoking.	I trust life and calmly allow it to be.

Record here the outcome you are realizing through your spiritual mind treatment:

Developing Your Spiritual Mind Treatment for Addiction

The following five pages are for your use in journaling about each step of your spiritual mind treatment and for exploring the language that is most meaningful to you. After you've done so, write your spiritual mind treatment on the page provided.

Recognition

Spirit is the essence of all that exists. Notice evidence of the presence of Spirit around you. Which spiritual qualities express the truth about your experience in the life area of Addiction? Recognize the presence of these qualities in your recognition step. Write your statement of recognition here, making it as sincere and meaningful as you can. See pages 17-18 for an explanation of this step of spiritual mind treatment.

Unification

As you recognize the presence of Spirit all around you, begin now to become aware of your connection with Spirit. Feel your oneness with the qualities of Spirit. Sense these spiritual qualities in, as, and through your life. Write a statement here that expresses your awareness of your unity with Spirit. See page 19 for an explanation of this step of spiritual mind treatment.

Realization

Your statement of realization sets into motion a new cause which you experience as a new effect. By affirming the spiritual truth about you, and identifying with the spiritual qualities you wish to express, you establish these qualities in and as your experience. Write your statement of realization here, including details and feelings that make it real and vivid for you. Be clear, definite, and specific. Remember to state your realization positively and to use the present tense. See pages 20-21 for an explanation of this step of spiritual mind treatment.

Thanksgiving

Giving thanks reinforces your sense of having received and accepted something. Here, with deep conviction, express your gratitude that your issue in the life area of Addiction is now resolved and that your healing is already established as a new cause. See pages 22–23 for an explanation of this step of spiritual mind treatment.

Release

Releasing your spiritual mind treatment directs the creative power of universal Mind, or law, to fulfill the new cause presented to it. With complete faith in the unfailing power of law, you present your new cause to be realized. You let it go, knowing it is done. Write your statement of release here. See pages 24–25 for an explanation of this step of spiritual mind treatment.

Your Spiritual Mind Treatment for Addiction

Combined together, the statements you have written on the previous five pages comprise your complete spiritual mind treatment for the life area of Addiction. Review your statements to be sure they evoke a deep feeling and conviction in you. Also make sure that the statements you have written for each of the steps of spiritual mind treatment fulfill the intended purpose of that step. Express the essence of each step of your spiritual mind treatment here.

When you are ready, write your statements here:

Recognition:

Unification:

Realization:

Thanksgiving:

Release:

See pages 30-31 for suggestions on what to do now that you have completed your spiritual mind treatment for the life area of Addiction.

Example of a Spiritual Mind Treatment for Addiction

The spiritual mind treatment is intended as a guide only. The effectiveness of your spiritual mind treatment is enhanced when you use words and statements that have the most meaning for you.

Problem to be addressed: Overeating as a way to cope with low self-esteem
Outcome: Feeling valued and worthy, release of need for food as comfort

Recognition:
Good is evident all around and everywhere, and this good is present in and through all. It is the source of all. Good lives in and through every form of life and activity that exists. Recognizing this truth, I am convinced of the unlimited, universal and omnipresent nature of infinite Spirit. I know that good is in all and through all.

Unification:
Knowing that good is in all and through all, I am aware right now that I am inseparably connected with it. I know that I am part of the infinite and perfect Spirit, and I enter into this awareness fully. I am one with the perfect goodness everywhere present.

Realization:
I realize that the spiritual truth about me is that as an expression of infinite being I am whole, perfect, and complete. Whatever sense of inadequacy or limitation I may have had is now replaced with a deep realization of my connection with an infinite power and presence, and I now release all belief in anything that contradicts this truth. I realize instead the truth of my nature as a center in infinite Spirit. I am always able to access the well-being, strength, power, and love of Spirit, because those qualities are my true nature and I can never be separate or apart from my true nature. Feeling valued and worthy, I release all need for comfort from overeating. Balance is easily established in every area of my life. I am safe and secure, and all is well. I feel joyous and free.

Thanksgiving:
For this realization I now give deep thanks and appreciation, knowing that I am made new through it. With a grateful heart I accept the truth that I am a whole and perfect expression of Spirit, and I embrace this truth fully.

Release:

I now release this treatment into the activity of the law of Mind, knowing that my word is fulfilled right now. It is done, and so it is.

LIFE DIRECTION

"We as individuals each have our own thoughts, feelings, hopes, aspirations, and desires, and each is directly and intimately connected with the one Divine Life, Energy, and Power. Each of us is a fountain of Life. There is a God-pressure back of each one of us, seeking outlet through our thoughts and acts."

—Ernest Holmes

Renewal is on ongoing process. There is always a greater good seeking to express. A concern about the direction of your life is a sign of your openness to the new experiences and greater self-awareness that this process of expansion brings. The urge to do something worthwhile and meaningful comes along. There is a readiness for spiritual deepening. You feel called to express more fully who you are, to bring forth the gifts and abilities within you, and to make a difference.

As exciting as this search can be, it can also be a time of baffling and uncomfortable change. Your former way of life may not seem as satisfying to you as it once did. Goals and values that were previously acceptable to you may no longer feel right. You may feel that your world is falling apart around you. In the midst of this confusion and turmoil, your deep self is being brought forth. A greater expression of who you are is emerging. Something within you is seeking to be realized.

It is Spirit within you, the essence of your being, which is ever urging you toward a fuller expression of who you truly are. Guidance comes to you as you open to the presence of Spirit and listen to your deep self. A vision or dream lives in your inner being. You can allow it to guide and direct you. Use spiritual mind treatment to identify your true self as Spirit and to realize your inherent qualities of guidance, inspiration, creativity, and fulfillment.

Know that you have a unique and valuable contribution to make in the world and that you activate the principle of attraction when you affirm and accept for yourself the meaningful life direction that is right for you.

Ideas for Contemplation:

"When we open to inspiration, the ideas for our life held in the Mind of God begin to live and express through us. We begin to be able to articulate them and to live and embody and reveal them. The feeling we have is that we have come home. We are fulfilling our heart's desire. Our heart's desire is about expressing ourselves, allowing our latent talents, gifts, and abilities to become actualized."

—Michael Bernard Beckwith

"A great number of people don't know what to do with their lives. I always refer them back to the idea that there is a divine plan for them and that if they will open their mind to this idea and ask divine intelligence to reveal to them the next step in the divine plan for their lives, then often the way is opened for a new unfolding to take place."

—Catherine Ponder

"I'm aware that each of us is sent here on an extraordinary mission, on an incredible assignment, and if we would but take up that assignment our whole life will change."

—Neale Donald Walsch

"When you are impregnated with a vision, the universe will not allow you to ignore it."

—Iyanla Vanzant

Contemplate these ideas. How do you feel about them? Do these ideas open you to new ways of thinking? Are you seeing ways in which limiting beliefs have affected your experience? Record below any new awareness or insights regarding your beliefs in the life area of Life Direction:

Clarifying the Issue

You have become aware of limiting beliefs and are opening to new ways of thinking about your experience in the life area of Life Direction. Use this list of statements to clarify the particular issues you want to heal through spiritual mind treatment. Circle the issues that apply to you. Write at the bottom of this page any additional issues not listed here.

I feel that life is passing me by.

My life doesn't seem to have much meaning.

I'm not accomplishing anything.

There's no enjoyment to living.

I'm confused about what to do with my life.

I'm not living up to my potential.

Nothing feels satisfying or worthwhile to me.

I'm afraid to make changes in my life.

I'm not sure what really interests me.

Now that I'm retired, I don't know what to do.

My life feels like it has gone stale.

I keep trying new things but nothing works.

Without my children at home I feel lost.

I want to be of service but don't know what to do.

I am uncertain about which career to pursue.

I can't seem to stay motivated.

I'm just marking time.

Other:

The Truth About You

Behind an experience of limitation is a belief in limitation. You can replace limiting beliefs by affirming the spiritual truth about you. In the list on the right are statements of spiritual truth. Use them as guides in stating the outcome you desire to realize through your spiritual mind treatment. At the bottom of the page, write the outcome you are realizing. Then use the following pages for the five steps of your spiritual mind treatment. An example of a spiritual mind treatment in the life area of Life Direction is on pages 155-156.

If you have been saying:	*Now begin to say:*
I'm not using my full potential.	I find new ways to express my gifts.
My life isn't going anywhere.	My life is active and purposeful.
There really isn't much to live for.	I am grateful for every new day.
The days all seem the same to me.	I experience the wonder of life.
My life doesn't have any direction.	I have a meaningful focus to my life.
I have trouble setting goals.	I am clear about what I want to do.
I can't get enthusiastic about anything.	I enjoy being alive.
I don't feel needed.	I am valued by myself and by others.
I never do anything different.	I find new ways to enjoy life.
I'm afraid to make changes.	I am safe in the midst of change.
I feel that life is passing me by.	I participate readily in new activities.
Without a job I don't know what to do.	I am guided to express in new ways.
Making choices is hard for me.	I am confident and decisive.
I feel alone and useless.	My life has a unique purpose.

Record here the outcome you are realizing through your spiritual mind treatment:

Developing Your Spiritual Mind Treatment for Life Direction

The following five pages are for your use in journaling about each step of your spiritual mind treatment and for exploring the language that is most meaningful to you. After you've done so, you will write your spiritual mind treatment on the page provided.

Recognition

Spirit is the essence of all that exists. Notice evidence of the presence of Spirit around you. Which spiritual qualities express the truth about your experience in the life area of Life Direction? Recognize the presence of these qualities in your recognition step. Write your statement of recognition here, making it as sincere and meaningful as you can. See pages 17-18 for an explanation of this step of spiritual mind treatment.

Unification

As you recognize the presence of Spirit all around you, begin now to become aware of your connection with Spirit. Feel your oneness with the qualities of Spirit. Sense these spiritual qualities in, as, and through your life. Write a statement here that expresses your awareness of your unity with Spirit. See page 19 for an explanation of this step of spiritual mind treatment.

Realization

Your statement of realization sets into motion a new cause which you experience as a new effect. By affirming the spiritual truth about you, and identifying with the spiritual qualities you wish to express, you establish these qualities in and as your experience. Write your statement of realization here, including details and feelings that make it real and vivid for you. Be clear, definite, and specific. Remember to state your realization positively and to use the present tense. See pages 20-21 for an explanation of this step of spiritual mind treatment.

Thanksgiving

Giving thanks reinforces your sense of having received and accepted something. Here, with deep conviction, express your gratitude that your issue in the life area of Life Direction is now resolved and that your healing is already established. See pages 22-23 for an explanation of this step of spiritual mind treatment.

Release

Releasing your spiritual mind treatment directs the creative power of universal Mind, or law, to fulfill the new cause presented to it. With complete faith in the unfailing power of law, you let it go, knowing that a new cause is set in motion. You know it is done. Write your statement of release here. See pages 24–25 for an explanation of this step of spiritual mind treatment.

Spiritual Mind Treatment for Life Direction

Combined together, the statements you have written on the previous five pages comprise your complete spiritual mind treatment for the life area of Life Direction. Review your statements to be sure they evoke a deep feeling and conviction in you. Also make sure that the statements you have written for each of the steps of spiritual mind treatment fulfill the intended purpose of that step. Express the essence of each step of your spiritual mind treatment here.

When you are ready, write your statements here:

Recognition:

Unification:

Realization:

Thanksgiving:

Release:

See pages 30–31 for suggestions on what to do now that you have completed your spiritual mind treatment for the life area of Life Direction.

Example of a Spiritual Mind Treatment for Life Direction

The following spiritual mind treatment is intended as a guide only. The effectiveness of your spiritual mind treatment is enhanced when you use words and statements that have the most meaning for you.

Problem to be addressed: Feeling adrift and without purpose
Outcome: A sense of purpose in my life and guidance in knowing what to do

Recognition:
There is only one infinite intelligence, the first cause and ultimate source of all that is. The universe is one perfectly harmonious presence and power, of which everything is a necessary part and in which everything expresses according to a perfect pattern.

Unification:
I am one with this infinite intelligence. All of the knowledge and power of infinite intelligence is within me and operates through me. I am immersed in the all-knowing, all-powerful life. Right now I consciously identify myself with this life and with the order, guidance, and harmony that are its true nature. I am an individualized center in the one Mind.

Realization:
Everything I think, say, and do is governed by an infinite intelligence. I align my thinking with the perfect order and harmony of Spirit, allowing a renewed sense of purpose to guide me. I know what to do and how to do it. I feel intuitively led to the right endeavors and activities. A creative spirit fills me and motivates me. I am free of all doubt and confusion. I experience clarity of purpose and I have the energy to follow through with that purpose. Knowing that I am an expression of Spirit, I go forward with confidence and a peaceful awareness of being guided. The infinite intelligence within me is awakened and active in my mind. My life is a great adventure, and I enjoy my life each and every day. The guidance of Spirit within me is gentle and true. I experience this guidance with deep assurance of its rightness for me, and I act on it easily and confidently.

Thanksgiving:
I thank the infinite intelligence for this realization, for this word of power, which is filling me right now with a sense of purpose for my life. I give thanks for the perfect guidance of Spirit in my life.

Release:

Accepting a sense of purpose as already established within me, I relax and simply let go. My word is released now into the creative power of universal Mind, and it goes forth to be perfectly fulfilled. And so it is!

AGING

"People do not grow old when they are busy with the pleasures of living, the enjoyment, the expectation, the enthusiasm, and the thought of the more that is to come. Youth is not a time of life—it is a state of mind. You are as young as your faith, as old as your doubt; as young as your confidence, as old as your fear; as young as your hope, as old as your despair."

—Ernest Holmes

Aging is the natural progression of life. As the years pass, you move from less mature stages of life to ever greater, more evolved ones. Through the new experiences that come, you are gaining wisdom, understanding, and compassion. You are developing a sense that growth is happening. The mature years of living become a time of inner peace, gratitude, and strength, and they offer rich opportunities for joy and fulfillment.

By now you've had many successes and failures. You've had disappointments as well as celebrations. Your life has been busy. You may have experienced marriage, a career, perhaps children and family, travel and adventure. But now you are moving into a next stage of life and your focus is shifting. While this is a special and valuable time of renewal for you, you may be feeling uncertain about the future. You may have concerns about such issues as retirement, health, financial resources, companionship, or physical vitality.

If you are experiencing any of these or other concerns related to aging, begin now to recognize the presence of Spirit in, as, and through you and your life. Spirit is eternal and it is everywhere present. You are that eternal Spirit in expression. With this idea in mind, realize and accept that growing older does not mean lack or limitation for you. It means ever evolving into the greater self that you are as Spirit, as a part of infinite life.

The presence and power of good are eternally within you, so be excited about what is in store for you. Let go of negative ideas about aging and embrace the prospect of ongoing expansion and expression. Choose the spiritual qualities you wish to realize for yourself. You have the ability to attract a fulfilling, vibrant life.

Ideas for Contemplation

"Just smiling goes a long way toward making you feel better about life. And when you feel better about life, your life is better. With an optimistic, positive attitude toward life, the possibilities for your second prime are tremendous."

—Art Linkletter

"As little children, we are completely authentic. We never pretend to be what we are not. Our tendency is to play and explore, to live in the moment, to enjoy life. Nobody teaches us to be that way; we are born that way. This is our true nature."

—Don Miguel Ruiz

"When you put any kind of a label on anything you experience, you negate it because you become more focused on the label than on what the experience has to teach you."

—Wayne Dyer

"Individuals mature to the point where they can gain a clearer understanding of their childhood influences and how these influences have affected their lives since childhood. The value of this kind of understanding is that we can enhance the positive lines of development and break free from the negative ones."

—Marianne Williamson

Contemplate these ideas. How do you feel about them? Do these ideas open you to new ways of thinking? Are you seeing ways in which limiting beliefs have affected your experience? Record below any new awareness or insights regarding your beliefs in the life area of Aging:

Clarifying the Issue

You have become aware of limiting beliefs and are opening to new ways of thinking about your experience in the life area of Aging. Use this list of statements to clarify the particular issues you want to heal through spiritual mind treatment. Circle the issues that apply to you. Write at the bottom of this page any additional issues not listed here.

Growing older scares me.

I'm not ready for retirement.

I'll never be able to remarry at my age.

I'm afraid of losing my independence.

I won't have enough money to live on.

I'm not as attractive as I used to be.

I'm afraid of serious health problems.

No one will be there to take care of me.

Younger people get all the promotions.

I'm not able to do the things I used to do.

I feel depressed a lot of the time.

I'm afraid of getting asked to retire.

My children don't have time for me.

My energy isn't what it used to be.

I don't feel needed anymore.

My body doesn't recover like it used to.

Other:

The Truth About You

Behind an experience of limitation is a belief in limitation. You can replace limiting beliefs by affirming the spiritual truth about you. In the list on the right are statements of spiritual truth. Use them as guides in stating the outcome you desire to realize through your spiritual mind treatment. At the bottom of the page, write the outcome you are realizing. Then use the following pages for the five steps of your spiritual mind treatment. An example of a spiritual mind treatment in the life area of Aging is found on pages 167-168.

If you have been saying:	*Now begin to say:*
The older I am, the slower I get.	I am energetic and vital.
Growing older scares me.	I find new sources of fulfillment.
Life seems empty with the children gone.	I have new interests to challenge me.
I'm not ready for retirement.	I am creating a life I enjoy.
I'm afraid of becoming dependent.	Life supports me in a way I enjoy.
My body is getting frail.	I am strong and vital.
I'm depressed about the loss of friends.	New experiences come along for me.
Promotions are going to younger people.	I am valued for my experience.
I can't find a spouse at my age.	I have a fulfilling relationship.
I'm afraid of being laid off.	My needs are met and I am secure.
I lack the energy I need to get things done.	I accomplish things easily.
My life is always the same every day.	There are exciting new things to do.
I'm not as attractive as I used to be.	Who I am inwardly is attractive.
I am troubled by regrets.	I release the past and enjoy today.
There's nothing left to live for.	I am here for a unique purpose.

Record here the outcome you are realizing through your spiritual mind treatment:

Developing Your Spiritual Mind Treatment for Aging

The following five pages are for your use in journaling about each step of your spiritual mind treatment and for exploring the language that is most meaningful to you. After you've done so, you will write your spiritual mind treatment on the page provided.

Recognition

Spirit is the essence of all that exists. Notice evidence of the presence of Spirit around you. Which spiritual qualities express the truth about your experience in the life area of Aging? Recognize the presence of these qualities in your recognition step. Write your statement of recognition here, making it as sincere and meaningful as you can. See pages 17-18 for an explanation of this step of spiritual mind treatment.

Unification

As you recognize the presence of Spirit all around you, begin now to become aware of your connection with Spirit. Feel your oneness with the qualities of Spirit. Sense these spiritual qualities in, as, and through your life. Write a statement here that expresses your awareness of your unity with Spirit. See page 19 for an explanation of this step of spiritual mind treatment.

Realization

Your statement of realization sets into motion a new cause which you experience as a new effect. By affirming the spiritual truth about you and identifying with the spiritual qualities you wish to express, you establish these qualities in and as your experience. Write your statement of realization here, including details and feelings that make it real and vivid for you. Be clear, definite, and specific. Remember to state your realization positively and to use the present tense. See pages 20-21 for an explanation of this step of spiritual mind treatment.

Thanksgiving

Giving thanks reinforces your sense of having received and accepted something. Here, with deep conviction, express your gratitude that your issue in the life area of Aging is now resolved and that your healing is already established. See pages 22-23 for an explanation of this step of spiritual mind treatment.

Release

Releasing your spiritual mind treatment directs the creative power of universal Mind, or law, to fulfill the new cause presented to it. With complete faith in the unfailing power of law, you let it go, knowing that a new cause is set in motion. You know it is done. Write your statement of release here. See pages 24–25 for an explanation of this step of spiritual mind treatment.

Your Spiritual Mind Treatment for Aging

Combined together, the statements you have written on the previous five pages comprise your complete spiritual mind treatment for the life area of Aging. Review your statements to be sure they evoke a deep feeling and conviction in you. Also make sure that the statements you have written for each of the steps of spiritual mind treatment fulfill the intended purpose of that step. Express the essence of each step of your spiritual mind treatment here.

When you are ready, write your statements here:

Recognition:

Unification:

Realization:

Thanksgiving:

Release:

See pages 30–31 for suggestions on what to do now that you have completed your spiritual mind treatment for the life area of Aging.

Example of a Spiritual Mind Treatment for Aging

The following spiritual mind treatment is intended as a guide only. The effectiveness of your spiritual mind treatment is enhanced when you use words and statements that have the most meaning for you.

Problem to be addressed: Loss of vitality
Outcome: Physical vitality and energy

Recognition:
I consciously awaken to Spirit's presence, and I acknowledge the power and healing energy that vibrates in and through every muscle, blood vessel, bone, organ, and atom of my being. I see this energy and I feel the vibration. The life of Spirit flows through me with a profound power and energy. I know that infinite Spirit brought me into existence, and sustains and nurtures me at all times.

Unification:
Spirit is my very life. I know that I am one with an infinite presence. The healing energy of Spirit is present at every point in my physical being and communicates Itself in the movements and actions of my body. This presence knows only perfection and wholeness, and therefore my body is whole and complete.

Realization:
I realize the truth of wholeness and healing in any and all aspects of my body. Spirit's healing energy is flowing through me in this very instant. It strengthens every bone and muscle, and opens every cell to vitality. All suggestion of age and limitation is uprooted from my mind. I know in this moment that I am one with Spirit's energetic flow. Nothing hinders my movement. Nothing keeps me from doing all of those things that I enjoy. Nothing prevents me from delighting in life to the fullest. I am filled with perfect life.

Thanksgiving:
I am grateful for Spirit's life in and as me. I am grateful for life expressing in such a wonderful way as my life and all my activities. I give thanks for the opportunity to be here at this moment, to feel the divine energy, and participate in life to the fullest.

Release:

I now release this treatment into that eternal law that acknowledges my belief and says yes! I rest in complete assurance that what I have declared is now accomplished. The law works with infinite exactness and in this certainty I rest and allow it to be. And so it is.

DEATH AND DYING

"What we call death is only an expansion of the soul, an enlargement of experience, a gateway into higher expressions of life and truth."

—Ernest Holmes

Death is a topic that many people prefer not to talk about. But it doesn't need to be a depressing or frightening subject. You can find great benefit in considering what death is and what it means to you. You can also find support in releasing loved ones who have died. Perhaps the death of a loved one is still painful for you and you long for understanding and comfort. Or someone you love is close to death right now and you want guidance in how to help your loved one and then how to move on with your life when that time comes. Death is part of living, and life is always ongoing.

But even when it is viewed as a new beginning rather than as an ending, death of a loved one can still cause grief, sorrow, and loneliness. There may also be feelings of fear and anger, a sense of unfinished business. As your own death approaches, you may experience concerns about your care, finances, diminished ability to function, or the impact on family members. If you have any of these concerns, begin to lift your thoughts out of worry and loss. Allow a sense of peace to settle within and around you. Shift your thoughts toward a deep awareness of infinite life and recognize the presence of this life as your own life. The spiritual qualities that are true of infinite life are also true of you.

If you have felt loss and pain, begin to sense the comfort, peace, and freedom of Spirit. Your true essence is spiritual and the physical body is only something you use for a period of time. Your spiritual essence can never be destroyed. Death is not an end to life but simply a change of form. Death is natural, and you as well as your loved ones are an inseparable part of the wholeness and perfection of Spirit, which always knows exactly what to do, when to do it, and how to do it.

Explore any feelings of fear, sadness, guilt, or anger you are experiencing with regard to death or dying and allow yourself to release these feelings. Recognize the eternal presence of infinite life everywhere, in and through all, and allow the peace and love of Spirit to express in and through your life.

169

Ideas for Contemplation:

"I don't understand why suffering is there or why death is there—these are the mysteries of the universe that one encounters at the edge. But what I do understand about the universe is that it is beautiful and awesome."

—Ram Dass

"Since Spirit is all there is, the different areas of our experience are points along a continuum, not distinct and separate aspects of our being. The emotions are Spirit in disguise, and the physical body is also Spirit in disguise. Sometimes patients may be so secure in the experience of Spirit as something that is immortal and continues after the death of the physical body that they may not desire to have a physical healing."

—Deepak Chopra

"Whether death comes prematurely through illness or accident, or whether it comes through old age, death is always an opening. So a great opportunity comes whenever we face death. When a form dissolves, always something shines through that had been obscured by the form. This is the formless one life."

—Eckhart Tolle

Contemplate these ideas. How do you feel about them? Do these ideas open you to new ways of thinking? Are you seeing ways in which limiting beliefs have affected your experience? Record below any new awareness or insights regarding your beliefs in the life area of Death and Dying:

Clarifying the Issue

You have become aware of limiting beliefs and are opening to new ways of thinking about your experience in the life area of Death and Dying. Use this list of statements to clarify the particular issues you want to heal through spiritual mind treatment. Circle the issues that apply to you. Write at the bottom of this page any additional issues not listed here.

I am afraid of death.

I feel alone and abandoned.

I've experienced too much loss.

I'm afraid of pain in dying.

I don't feel finished with my life.

I don't want to leave my family.

I'm worried about medical costs.

My spouse won't know how to cope.

I don't want to be a burden to anyone.

I can't bear to have my child die.

I never told my parents that I loved them.

I'm angry that my loved one has died.

My financial affairs are in a bad state.

I can't go on without my spouse.

I've never really lived fully.

I miss my loved one terribly.

Other:

The Truth About You

Behind an experience of limitation is a belief in limitation. You can replace limiting beliefs by affirming the spiritual truth about you. In the list on the right are statements of spiritual truth. Use them as guides in stating the outcome you desire to realize through your spiritual mind treatment. At the bottom of the page, write the outcome you wish to express. Then use the following pages for the five steps of your spiritual mind treatment. An example of a spiritual mind treatment in the life area of Death and Dying is on pages 179-180.

If you have been saying:	*Now begin to say:*
I'm afraid of dying.	I trust life to be ongoing and eternal.
I'm angry that my loved one has died.	I accept anger as a natural response.
It's hard for me to talk about death.	I feel safe and supported.
I'm worried about medical costs.	The money I need is available to me.
I'd like to have done more with my life.	I am fulfilled and complete.
I'm afraid of losing my loved one.	My loved one is always with me.
I can't get over the grief I'm feeling.	I accept peace and healing.
I'm concerned about unfinished business.	Everything is just as it needs to be.
I'm worried about leaving my children.	My children are safe and cared for.
I never had the chance to say goodbye.	I accept closure with my loved one.
I'm sad and lonely with my spouse gone.	Love is always present with me.
I don't feel that my life has really mattered.	My life is valued by others.
I'd like to have accomplished more.	I accept the perfection of my life.
I feel bad that my spouse will be alone.	Our love continues to bring comfort.
I didn't say the things I should have said.	There is unspoken communication.

Record here the outcome you are realizing through your spiritual mind treatment:

Developing Your Spiritual Mind Treatment for Death and Dying

The following five pages are for your use in journaling about each step of your spiritual mind treatment and for exploring the language that is most meaningful to you. After you've done so, you will write your spiritual mind treatment on the page provided.

Recognition

Spirit is the essence of all that exists. Notice evidence of the presence of Spirit around you. Which spiritual qualities express the truth about your experience in the life area of Death and Dying? Recognize the presence of these qualities in your recognition step. Write your statement of recognition here, making it as sincere and meaningful as you can. See pages 17-18 for an explanation of this step of spiritual mind treatment.

Unification

As you recognize the presence of Spirit all around you, begin now to become aware of your connection with Spirit. Feel your oneness with the qualities of Spirit. Sense these spiritual qualities in, as, and through your life. Write a statement here that expresses your awareness of your unity with Spirit. See page 19 for an explanation of this step of spiritual mind treatment.

Realization

Your statement of realization sets into motion a new cause which you experience as a new effect. By affirming the spiritual truth about you, and identifying with the spiritual qualities you wish to express, you establish these qualities in and as your experience. Write your statement of realization here, including details and feelings that make it real and vivid for you. Be clear, definite, and specific. Remember to state your realization positively and to use the present tense. See pages 20-21 for an explanation of this step of spiritual mind treatment.

Thanksgiving

Giving thanks reinforces your sense of having received and accepted something. Here, with deep conviction, express your gratitude that your issue in the life area of Death and Dying is now resolved and that your healing is already established. See pages 22-23 for an explanation of this step of spiritual mind treatment.

Release

Releasing your spiritual mind treatment directs the creative power of universal Mind, or law, to fulfill the new cause presented to it. With complete faith in the unfailing power of law, you let it go, knowing that a new cause is set in motion. You know it is done. Write your statement of release here. See pages 24–25 for an explanation of this step of spiritual mind treatment.

Your Spiritual Mind Treatment for Death and Dying

Combined together, the statements you have written on the previous five pages comprise your complete spiritual mind treatment for the life area of Death and Dying. Review your statements to be sure they evoke a deep feeling and conviction in you. Also make sure that the statements you have written for each of the steps of spiritual mind treatment fulfill the intended purpose of that step. Express the essence of each step of your spiritual mind treatment here.

When you are ready, write your statements here:

Recognition:

Unification:

Realization:

Thanksgiving:

Release:

See pages 30-31 for suggestions on what to do now that you have completed your spiritual mind treatment for the life area of Death and Dying.

Example of a Spiritual Mind Treatment for Death and Dying

The following spiritual mind treatment is intended as a guide only. The effectiveness of your spiritual mind treatment is enhanced when you use words and statements that have the most meaning for you.

Problem to be addressed: Inability to accept the loss of my loved one
Outcome: Peaceful acceptance of the loss of my loved one

Recognition:
I know that there is one eternal life. It is all there is in the universe and it is infinite, invisible being, everywhere present, now and always—one creator and one creation. There is one ultimate reality, whole, perfect, complete. It is the presence and power of Spirit, expressing in, through, and as form.

Unification:
I now consciously sense and feel the presence of Spirit within me and as who I am. I know I am a creation of life and that I express life. There is no separation. I am one with Spirit. All of life is one with Spirit, which is always fully and completely present. The eternal life lives in me and in all people, always.

Realization:
Today I am living in an eternal present filled with an everlasting good and an abiding love. All in my life is peaceful. There is nothing unhappy or despairing that can remain in my consciousness. I no longer have any thoughts of loss or separation from my loved one. Everything that was good yesterday is still good today. I realize the eternal love and life in which I and my loved one are held. In this day there is no loss or sadness in my thoughts. I know that all is well and I accept my loved one's passing, because I know that Spirit is now and eternally present in, as, and through me as well as my loved one. I see the absolute perfection in my loved one's new life in Spirit. The physical body has moved on, but my loved one is always present in my heart because I know the true essence as Spirit lives on eternally. I sense his/her presence with me now, and I am at peace with the ongoing spiritual evolution of my loved one. I rejoice in his/her new expression.

Thanksgiving:
I give thanks for the peaceful sense of acceptance that fills me. I am grateful for all the good in my life.

Release:

Knowing that these are the words of Spirit and of life, I release them to the instantaneous activity of law and gratefully let this treatment be fulfilled completely and perfectly. And so it is.

PART FOUR
Conclusion

REST ASSURED

"I now accept the creative action of the words I have spoken as the law and the thing to which they are directed. They go forth into immediate fulfillment. Right now they are fully manifest. There is no delay, nor is there anything that can prevent them from now being fully and completely fulfilled in my experience. They are words of power and of good. I accept them. I know they are the truth of that which I am. In and through them Life goes forth anew into creation. It is now done, it is now complete. For this knowledge, for this understanding, I am grateful. I give thanks that this is so. I know and accept that there is One Life, that this Life is perfect, and that this Life is my life now. And so it is."

—Ernest Holmes

Learning is in the doing. As you work with the techniques you are learning, you are changing the main tendency of your thinking. You are shifting it toward a full, complete, and firm conviction of your oneness with that which is always whole and perfect—a conviction of your unity with Spirit.

Everything unlike the wholeness and perfection of Spirit, the universal all, is being eliminated from your thinking, because you are aligning your mind with the one Mind, or first cause. You are seeing beyond appearances to the inherent wholeness and perfection of all that exists, including you. You are changing old ways of thinking.

Old ways of thinking are nothing more than habits of behavior. Even when seemingly ingrained, they can be changed. As you conclude your work in *It Is About You*, consider if you are still holding on to any old ways of thinking, such as:

Reluctance to give up a problem's hidden benefit. Know that the benefits of healing the problem far outweigh any "payoff" from it.

Diminished expectations. See the greater possibilities for your life. Realize that more good is always available to you.

Low self-esteem. Feel the truth that you are worthy of success, love, and abundance. You are Spirit in expression.

Being lost without the problem. Your identity is your inherent nature as Spirit. Know that you are so much more than any problem you may be experiencing.

Fear of change. Be willing to venture into the unknown. Let go of any tendency to cling to the familiar if it is not fulfilling to you.

Fear of giving up control. Be willing to trust and to allow a greater good into your life.

If any of these old ideas apply in your case, allow them to dissolve so you can move forward fully and freely into a greater expression of who you truly are.

There is a creative power within you that you can use. Your mind is an individualized center in Spirit and your thought is acted upon by the creative power of Mind. By focusing on your oneness with Spirit, you establish a new cause, which is then fulfilled in your life through the creative power of Mind. Trust this power. Let it work in your life for good.

Your new thought shapes your outer experience. Your spiritual work consists not in trying to "force" the universal creative power to work. Rather, your spiritual work consists in knowing the truth of your oneness with Spirit and realizing the presence of Spirit in and as the particular condition you are addressing through your spiritual mind treatment.

Ernest Holmes says, "It is done unto us! We do not *coerce,* we do not *create* the power, but we must let this Great Power operate through us." So there is no coercion in this process. You are not willing anything to happen; things are brought into being through the realization and acceptance of your spiritual nature.

To realize and accept your spiritual nature is to mentally see the perfect pattern beyond any imperfect appearance. The universal creative power is always present and always acting to bring new forms into outer expression.

As an individualized center in Spirit, you are an instrument of Spirit's expression. You are letting the power of creative Mind flow through you in a new way. You may depend completely on this power. It is always responsive. It always works. Through whatever means or through whatever process the new manifestation unfolds, it does unfold. The natural work of Mind is to fulfill your mental image or pattern. Your role in the process is simply to stay attuned to the highest you can conceive—simply to know, to believe, and to expect.

In doing spiritual mind treatment to heal and clear unwanted conditions in your life, give your words the vital, dynamic feeling that makes them come alive in and as your experience. Have conviction. Align your thinking with that which is true of Spirit. Wholeness is the truth of who you are.

Ernest Holmes writes, "We should strive toward a perfect vision, a perfect conception. We should expand our thought until it realizes all good, and then cut right through all that *appears* to be, and use this Almighty Power for definite purposes."

When you release your new thought to the creative power of Mind, you are dissolving the negative appearance in a condition by recognizing only perfection. You have released a new thought, a perfect conception, into the creative soil of Mind and you may rest assured that your new thought is becoming a reality in your life.

Use the power for good that is within you. Expect great results. Expect to experience positive changes in your life. These changes for the better are already underway.

Life is an exciting adventure, and it holds the promise of much more than you have yet realized. Life is an open door to whatever you decide to let it be. It *is* all about you.

I Am Entering into a New Life

"Today I am entering into a new life. The doorway of opportunity is open wide before me. Something within me is alert and aware. My will, my thought, and my imagination feel and sense new opportunities for self-expression. I identify myself with success. I am one with it. New ideas and new ways of doing things come to me.

I have complete confidence that I recognize opportunity when it presents itself. I know what to do under every circumstance and in every situation. There is a deep feeling within me that all is well. I am ready and willing to give the best I have to life, and I know the best that life has comes back to me.

Believing that Divine Power is back of every constructive thought, that I live in a Divine Presence which flows through everything, and that I am guided by an infinite Intelligence which knows everything, I live this day in complete assurance. I live this day in complete happiness. And I expect that tomorrow will reveal an increasing unfoldment, an increasing revelation of that good which is eternally available for every person."

And so it is.

—Ernest Holmes

More Resources

Books by Ernest Holmes:

365 Days of Richer Living. Los Angeles: Science of Mind Publishing, 2006.

365 Science of Mind. New York: Tarcher/Putnam, 2001.

Can We Talk to God? Deerfield Beach, FL: Health Communications, 1999.

Creative Ideas. Los Angeles: Science of Mind Publishing, 2005.

Creative Mind and Success. New York: Tarcher/Putnam, 1997.

Creative Mind. Los Angeles: Science of Mind Publishing, 2003.

The Essential Ernest Holmes. New York: Tarcher/Putnam, 2002.

How to Change Your Life. Deerfield Beach, FL: Health Communications, 1999.

How to Use the Science of Mind. Los Angeles: Science of Mind Publishing, 2002.

Living the Science of Mind. Camarillo, CA: DeVorss & Company, 1991.

Love and Law. New York: Tarcher/Putnam, 2001.

The Science of Mind. New York: Tarcher/Putnam, 1998.

The Art of Life. New York: Tarcher/Putnam, 2004.

This Thing Called You. New York: Tarcher/Penguin, 2004.

The Voice Celestial. Los Angeles, Science of Mind Publishing, 2004.

What Religious Science Teaches. Los Angeles, Science of Mind Publishing, 2003.

Words That Heal Today. Deerfield Beach, FL: Health Communications, 1999.

Concordance:
Concordance to the Science of Mind. Martha Ann Stewart and Albert G. Lowe. Los Angeles: Science of Mind Publishing, 2007.

Books about Ernest Holmes:

Armor, Reginald C. *That Was Ernest: The Story of Ernest Holmes and the Religious Science Movement.* Camarillo, CA: DeVorss Publications, 1999.

Holmes, Fenwicke. *Ernest Holmes: His Life and Times.* New York: Dodd, Mead & Company, 1970.

Leo, Marilyn. *In His Company: Ernest Holmes Remembered.* Camarillo, CA: M. Leo Presents, 2007.

Vahle, Neal. *Open at the Top: The Life of Ernest Holmes.* Mill Valley, CA: Open View Press, 1993.

These books by and about Ernest Holmes are available from DeVorss & Co., and can be ordered by calling 800-382-6121 or by visiting their website: www.devorss.com. Amazon.com., and the Barnes and Noble site, www.bn.com., also carry the above titles.

Periodicals:
Science of Mind magazine
Read *Science of Mind* for the best in contemporary spirituality. Founded in 1927 by Ernest Holmes, *Science of Mind* provides interviews with modern spiritual leaders, insightful, practical essays and an inspirational passage for every day of the year. To subscribe to *Science of Mind*, call 800-247-6463 or visit www.science-ofmind.com.

Creative Thought magazine
Creative Thought is the monthly magazine published by Religious Science International. For more information, call (509) 624-7000.

Websites:
www.scienceofmind.com
www.religiousscience.org

Science of Mind Centers:

See the directories in *Science of Mind* magazine (for United Centers for Spiritual Living, www.religiousscience.org) and in *Creative Thought* (Religious Science International, www.rsintl.org) for information on a science of mind center near you.

Spiritual Mind Treatment:

For affirmative prayer 24 hours a day, call the World Ministry of Prayer at (800) 421-9600, or go to www.wmop.org.

About Ernest Holmes

Ernest Holmes (1887-1960), who developed the Science of Mind philosophy on which this workbook is based, is known internationally as one of the twentieth century's outstanding spiritual teachers. A lifelong student of philosophy and religion, he developed a practical approach to successful living, called the Science of Mind. It combines his own spiritual insights with essential principles from the world's enduring religious and spiritual traditions.

Ernest Holmes wrote many books, including his classic *The Science of Mind,* as well as *How to Use the Science of Mind, Creative Ideas, This Thing Called You,* and *Creative Mind and Success.* He also founded *Science of Mind* magazine and the United Church of Religious Science, now renamed United Centers for Spiritual Living. Another organization, Religious Science International, also presents the ideas developed by Ernest Holmes.

Through lectures, study courses, radio and television programs, classes, and his numerous books, Ernest Holmes has introduced many thousands of people around the world to the life-changing concepts of the Science of Mind philosophy.

About the Author

Kathy Juline is a former editor of *Science of Mind* magazine and regularly contributes articles and interviews to that publication. She edited a selection of writings by Ernest Holmes entitled *365 Science of Mind*, published in 2001 by Tarcher/Putnam. Juline lives in San Clemente, California, and can be reached at kathyjuline@cox.net.